IN HIS LIKENESS SERIES™

## GOD'S PURPOSE FOR YOUR LIFE

# NANCY MISSLER

# Table of Contents

**Chapter**                                    **Page**

Foreward................................................. 5

Preface .................................................. 7

Introduction ......................................... 11

Warning: Enemies Game Plan ............... 21

1. What is God's Plan? ............................ 25

2. So, What's the Problem?...................... 51

3. A Visual Picture of the Problem............ 87

4. How to Choose to Follow the Spirit....... 119

5. How to be Cleansed by the Spirit .......... 153

6. How to Worship the Spirit .................... 179

7. How to Abide in the Spirit..................... 197

8. How to Walk in the Spirit ...................... 245

Bibliography .......................................... 275

"But we all, with open face beholding as in a glass the glory of the Lord, are changed into the same image from glory to glory, even as by the Spirit of the Lord." (2 Corinthians 3:18)

# Foreward

"It's the little foxes that ruin the vine."

So wrote Solomon in one of his books contained in that ancient collection of divine wisdom that our Jewish friends call the *Tanakh* and that we Christians call the Old Testament. I was reminded of the enduring value of this wise King's counsel as I read Nancy Missler's delightful new book **Reflections of His Image**. That's because **Reflections** reminds me that there is no shortcut to maturity.

As I read and re-read **Reflections**, I'm reminded that, in a similar vein, what matters along the journey is not the vision, dream or other Christian experience that predicts or describes the journey. Rather, *what matters is the perseverance that leads to the development of a truly eternal character.* In and of itself, no vision, dream or other experience can bring about that precious commodity within the life of any man or woman. *Christ-likeness is the only commodity that any mortal man or woman can carry of out this world into eternity.*

**Reflections** reminded me over and over again of the limited value Christians should place on looking to the future. *Now* is the season to see God work maturity into our character.  We must be in love with the One who shows Himself powerful enough to save and to deliver–and to forge our souls into mettle worthy of His service.

If you have lost your way on the journey of life for a season, ***Reflections of His Image: God's Purpose for Your Life*** may be just the thing to set you back on that sure and certain, straight and narrow road, headed to the place to which you were destined from the creation of the world.

*William Welty*

William P.  Welty, M.Div.
Executive Director of The ISV Foundation
Translators of the Holy Bible: International Standard Version®

# Preface
## "Only One Turned Back"

"And it came to pass, as He went to Jerusalem, that He passed through the midst of Samaria and Galilee. And as He entered into a certain village, there met Him *ten* men that were lepers, which stood afar off. And they lifted up their voices, and said, Jesus, Master, have mercy on us. And when He saw them, He said unto them, go show yourselves unto the priests. And it came to pass, that, as they went, they were cleansed. *And [only] one of them, when he saw that he was healed, turned back and with a loud voice glorified God. And fell down on* **his** *face at His feet, giving Him thanks...* And Jesus answering said, were there not ten cleansed? *But where are the nine*? There are not found that returned to give glory to God, except this stranger.'" (Luke 17:11-18)

Jesus is saying here that of the ten healed only *one* turned back, gave thanks and glorified the Lord. Why? Where were the other nine?

To me, this is shocking!

But we must ask ourselves the very same question. How many of us who have been made whole by Christ have turned back, given thanks and are now glorifying Him in all we do? As Christians, we want to be personally energized by the Lord and have our prayers answered. But, many of us are not interested in humbling ourselves, sacrificing our wills and lives and showing forth <u>His</u> glory to others.

---

Yesterday Chuck and I received word about a dear Christian brother of ours (a childhood friend), who has been stricken with a brain hemorrhage. His wife told us that the prognosis is very bleak. This incident hits close to home because it makes us realize how very short life is here on earth. As young Christians, we don't think much about death or dying–it's a far off reality that we're not really interested in spending too much time contemplating. But as we grow older and we see those we love, and grew up with, fall sick and eventually die, it forces us to consider our own mortality. When all is said and done and we stand at eternity's threshold, how many of us will have the confidence that we–just like that one Samaritan man who fell down on his face and with a loud voice glorified God–have done our best to glorify God and show forth His image to the world? How many of us, at that point, will fall on our faces and give thanks for the life He gave us? Yes, and even thanks for the tragedies, the hard times and tears, because those were the times that made us more like Him.

I, personally, want to be like the *one* leper who turned back, fell on his face and with a loud voice thanked and glorified God. And the only way I know how to do that is to continue to live all He has taught me over the past 50 years that I have walked with Him. A dear prisoner recently wrote me and called my writings *"the knowledge of experience."* I loved that and I think I understand exactly what he meant. When you've experienced the hard times, the testings and the pruning, you gain knowledge from them that many others may not have. Thus, you can authentically write about them– *from "the knowledge of experience."*

With that in mind, the following book is humbly written as a personal thank-you to my precious Lord and to glorify Him who has given me the "knowledge of life," and that very abundantly. (John 10:10b)

"I will praise Thee, O Lord my God, with all my heart: and I will glorify Thy Name for evermore." (Psalm 86:12)

# Introduction
## What is God's Purpose for our Lives?

2 Corinthians 3:18 is a Scripture that perfectly describes God's purpose for us as Christians: "We all... are [being] changed into the same image from glory to glory, even as by the Spirit of the Lord."

Let me tell you one of my favorite stories and see if it doesn't bring this Scripture to life. This is a true incident that happened years ago between a dear Christian friend of mine named Melody and her mom, Florence (who was not a believer).

Florence had gone to the same hairdresser for years. Every time she came back from her appointment, she would tell her daughter, "Honey, you have to meet Susie my hairdresser. *You both look exactly alike.*" Finally, Melody was home for a long enough visit that she consented to making an appointment with Susie. Needless to say, she was very anxious to meet this woman who supposedly "looked exactly like her."

When Melody walked into the hair salon and was introduced to Susie, she was startled to see no physical resemblance between them at all. Melody was very short, with a dark complexion and dark hair. She was very pretty with rounded features. Susie, on the other hand, was very tall, blonde, skinny and had angular features. There were absolutely <u>no</u> physical similarities between them at all.

Of course, the mom was very excited to introduce them to each other. All three talked for a few minutes and then the mom made her apologies and left. Melody stood there awkwardly for a moment, and then hesitatingly asked Susie if her mom had also told her that they looked alike. "Of course," Susie said, "for years she has told me that I look exactly like you. I am shocked and surprised to meet you." "Me too," said Melody.

While Melody was getting her hair cut, shampooed and set, she and Susie had a chance to share some details about their lives. It turned out they were both Christians and both were truly committed to living for the Lord. Melody's mom, however, was <u>not</u> a believer. After thinking about it for a while, it dawned on them that the reason Melody's unsaved mom thought they looked alike was probably because *she saw Jesus' image in both of them*. It was *His* character, *His* Life and *His* Image that the mom evidently saw. Physically, Melody and Susie didn't resemble each other in the least, but spiritually, they had the very same image.

I love this story because it shows the power we carry around with us when we allow Christ to live His Life out through us. Scripture tells us Christ is to be magnified (reflected, glorified and shine forth) in our bodies and that whatever we do; we are to do for *His* glory.[1] 1 Peter 4: 11 summarizes it by saying, "If any man speak, let him speak as the oracles of God; if anyone minister, let him do it as of the ability which God giveth." Why? So *"that God in all things may be glorified."* [2]

This is God's purpose for our lives.

## Transformed into His Likeness

We were created for God and His purposes, thus, our fulfillment will only come when we align ourselves with His design and His intentions.

Most of you who have picked up this book, I am assuming, are Christians. If you are, then ask yourself these questions. (Try to be honest with yourself!) ***When people look at you, do they see the characteristics of Christ?*** Like Melody's mom, do they see His image? Is your life a reflection of His Love, joy and peace?

In one of his recent *Times Square Pulpit Series* articles, David Wilkerson said: "If I am not Christ-like at heart–if I'm not becoming noticeably more like Him– then I have totally missed God's purpose for my life. It doesn't matter what I accomplish for His kingdom. If I miss this one purpose, I have lived, preached and yes, striven in vain."

---

[1]  1 Corinthians10:31; Philippians 1:20
[2]  Psalm 115:1; 1 Corinthians 6:20; Romans 15:6

And he continues, "Now, I help pastor what would be called a mega-church. I conduct minister's conferences around the world, preaching to thousands at a time. I founded Teen Challenge, a Christian rehabilitation ministry for alcoholics and drug addicts, which now has 500 centers worldwide. I've written some twenty books, helped establish a Bible school, set up a home for abandoned mothers and their children. I've had honors heaped on me. *But if this isn't my wife's testimony*–if she has a secret pain in her heart, thinking, 'My husband isn't the man of God he pretends to be'–*then everything in my life is vain.* All my works–the preaching, the accomplishments, the charitable giving, the many travels–amount to nothing. I am a withering, useless branch that doesn't bear the 'fruit of Christ-likeness.' Jesus will cause others to see the death in me, and I'll be worth little to His kingdom."

He finishes by saying: "God's purpose is fulfilled in me only by what I am becoming in Him. Christ-likeness isn't about what I *do* for the Lord, but about *how I'm being transformed into His likeness.*"[3]

## The Holy Spirit Transforms Us

Christ gave us His Holy Spirit in order to help with this transformation. The Holy Spirit is the third person of the Trinity and He is our comforter, counselor, helper, supporter, advisor, advocate and ally.[4,5] When we became

---

3    David Wilkerson's April '05 *Times Square Church Pulpit Series*
4    Packer, *Keep in Step with the Spirit*, pages 44, 56
5    Ephesians 1:3-13; 2:18; 1 Corinthians 12:4-6; 2 Corinthians 13:14

believers, God's Spirit came to indwell us as a pledge, a seal or a mark of ownership, indicating that we now belong to God.[6]

This Spirit then, is the One that sets about conforming us into Christ's image. (2 Corinthians 3:18) His job is to make Christ's presence known to us first and, then through us, to others.

J. I. Packer in his wonderful book *Keep in Step with the Spirit*, says, "On the night of His betrayal Jesus said of the Spirit: 'He will glorify Me...' (John 16:14) That is, He shall make Me glorious in people's eyes by making them aware of the Father's glory in Me. That basic definition of what the Spirit was sent to do gives us a comprehensive directional frame of reference within which the whole of the Spirit's new covenant ministry should be seen, and apart from which no feature of that ministry can be adequately understood."

## An Example: A Withering Useless Branch

The Bible tells us that no matter what difficulties we face, we are to bear Christ's likeness in all circumstances. We are to edify and encourage one another just as Jesus did, not tear each other down. God doesn't want us to just **have a revelation** of Christ, He wants us **to be a reproduction** of Christ.

---

[6]     2 Corinthians 1:22; Ephesians 1:13-14

This hits close to home because I just heard about an incident that recently happened to a very dear Christian friend of mine. For the last several years, my friend has had serious life threatening heart problems. A few months ago, she was again confined to the hospital with heart pains. One of the pastors at her church heard about her illness and came to the hospital to see her with the pretext of ministering to her. However, his real motive for coming was to confront her over some issues at church. The stress of this encounter precipitated a mild heart attack three days later.

Where is the fruit of Christ-likeness here? Where is the compassion, the edification and the encouragement that Jesus would have ministered?

If for some reason a confrontation is needed, then we not only must be sensitive to the Lord's timing in which to do it, but also the Christ-like character that it is given in. No matter what the circumstances were, I know Jesus would *never* have confronted and argued with someone who was recovering from a recent heart attack. Another time and place could easily have been set up to discuss whatever issues remained.

Unfortunately, this story is all too common among Christians these days. The hurt, devastation and feeling of betrayal left after an incident like this is crippling. What's going on here? Aren't we supposed to be lifting each other up? Aren't we supposed to be praying for one another and sharing one another's burdens?  That's what Jesus would do.  Scripture tells us that we are to reflect *Him* in <u>all</u> circumstances, no matter what the difficulties are.

As Wilkerson said, *if we are not Christ-like at heart* (and I will include in all our actions), *then we have totally missed God's purpose for our lives.*

## Our Purpose as Christians

The Bible tells us that our purpose is to be conformed into the image of Christ so that we can glorify Him in all we do.  "For whom He did foreknow, He also did predestinate *to be conformed to the image of His Son*." (Romans 8:29)

We are to comfort, encourage, edify and strengthen one another, as Jesus would do.  Yes, there will be times when we must confront one another in love and stand strong, but certainly not be so insensitive as to pick a fight in a hospital room!  1 John 4: 17 confirms: "Herein is our love made perfect, that we may have boldness in the day of judgment: because *as He is, so are we in this world.*"

Being conformed into Christ's image is the *goal* of the Christian life.  In other words, simply being *born in the spirit* at our new birth is **not** enough.  We need to learn how to *walk in the Spirit*, how to *show forth His Love* and how to *live His Life*. We need to put in our actions, what we already possess in our heart. This is the purpose of our existence as Christians. We are to be changed from the "inside out" and begin to reflect His likeness and His image.[7] We are to love with *His* Love;[8] share from *His* wisdom; walk in *His* power; extend *His* peace, patience and joy; and be *His* arms and legs to one another. In the above hospital example and the thousands of other ungodly incidents I hear about, where is God's Love? Where is His wisdom? Where is His compassion?

Again, we are made for God and our fulfillment in this life lies only in allowing Him to mold and sculpt us into His image. "Glorifying God" simply means reflecting His likeness in all we do. It means unlearning all our old ways of thinking and doing, and allowing Him to show forth, manifest and express His characteristics through us. It means removing every hindrance, every obstacle and every blockage in our life that quenches His Spirit, so that He may be clearly seen through us, just as the Father was perfectly seen through Jesus. As Hebrews 1: 3 says, "Jesus, who was "the brightness of His glory and the express image of His person."

Jesus even goes further and says in John 5:31, "If I bear witness of Myself, my witness is not true." Wow! If Jesus says this of Himself, oh my goodness, how much more it must be true for us! We are to bear witness of God's image, not our own.

---

7        Galatians 4:19; Romans 8:29
8        If you have read any of my other books on love, particularly *The Way of Agape*, you'll remember that God's Love has two sides to it: one side is a longsuffering and patient Love; the other side is a tough Love. Both sides make up God's unconditional Love. And, it's His wisdom that will tell us which type of Love to use for our individual circumstances.

# The Key to Revival

I am totally convinced that genuinely reflecting the Lord in all that we think, say and do is the key to revival. Seeing "living examples" of Christ is what will bring our sons and daughters, our friends and acquaintances to the Lord. When they see Christ's real Love, hear His supernatural wisdom and experience His power through us, they'll know that *yes, Jesus is real. He is alive. And He cares*! Nothing will bring others to saving knowledge of Christ faster than seeing genuine living examples. And nothing will turn them away quicker than phoniness and hypocrisy. Therefore, glorifying, manifesting and reflecting Christ in everything is our highest attainment in this life. It's the reason we were called, the purpose of our lives and what will bring others to Christ.

In order to evaluate your own progress towards this end, ask yourself these three simple questions: Does being a Christian make a difference in my life? Does Christ's character flow forth from me? Do others see the Love of Christ and the fruit of the Spirit in me?

Again, **God doesn't just want us *to have* a revelation of Christ, He wants us *to be* a reflection of Him.**

The question is: <u>*How*</u> *do we become a reproduction of Christ?* <u>How</u> are we conformed into His image? <u>What</u> must we do? <u>What</u> are the steps?

That's what this book is all about...

# Warning: Enemy's Game Plan

My name is Debbie Holland and I am the Manager of *The King's High Way* Ministries. I have worked with Nan for almost seven years and have proofread most all of her books. This one, however, is very different from all the rest. And that's why I am writing this warning!

There seems to be such a powerful conviction of the Holy Spirit that accompanies this writing, which the enemy will throw everything he can at you to persuade you not to read further. I've never experienced anything like it before. Every time I would get ready to read a chapter, some crisis would occur and I'd have to put it off. I'd set time aside in the evenings, but some disturbance would always happen that would prevent my reading further. I'd plan to commit time at work to read, but some business matter would always interfere. I didn't recognize this until half way through the book.

The Lord gave me understanding and showed me that the Biblical principles herein are the *key* to the Christian life and thus, the enemy is on a rampage. He desperately wants to stop the communication of these principles any way he can. The Lord showed me that if I would pray each time *before* reading, I would not only be blood-covered and protected from the enemy's attacks, but I would also be open to receive all I could from each chapter.

So as you read on, I encourage you to do the same. There is a short Scriptural prayer at the beginning of each chapter that will bind the enemy and help you to focus on what you are reading. By faith, say the prayer in your own words and put the armor of God on. The Lord will then protect you from the devil's blatant attacks, help keep your mind focused on what you are reading and as a result, your life will be changed.

Truly, "we wrestle not against flesh and blood, but against principalities, against powers, against the rulers of the darkness of this world, [and] against spiritual wickedness in high places." (Ephesians 6:12)

God's purpose for calling us as Christians is to be "conformed into His image" so that we might be able to walk by the Spirit and be genuine ***Reflections of His Image***.

# Warfare Prayer

Dearest Lord: I desire to be a "reflection of Your image," so that my family, friends and others will see You in me and want what I have. Therefore, I choose to give You anything in me that would prevent my hearing directly from Your Spirit. I present my body as a living sacrifice, holy and acceptable unto You, which is my reasonable service. And I choose *not* to be conformed to this world but to be transformed (into Your image) by the renewing of my mind, that I may prove what is Your good and acceptable and perfect will. (Romans 12:1-2)

I choose to *put on* the whole armor of God that I might be able to stand against the wiles of the enemy, having done all to stand strong. First of all, I choose to stand by **having my loins girt about with truth**... (Ephesians 6:13-14)

# Chapter One
## What is God's Plan?

In the beginning, man was created in the image and glory of God[9], but through Adam and Eve's sin, that image was lost and man fell short of his destiny.[10] Jesus, however, came to restore that destiny for us.[11] At our new birth–when we ask God's Spirit to come in and dwell in us–we are once again endowed with the nature of God in our hearts. But, bear in mind, this does *not* guarantee our being able to manifest that image of Christ out in our lives. Being "born of the Spirit" is <u>not</u> the same thing as "walking in the Spirit." There is a whole inner process of change that needs to take place *before* this transformation can happen. And that's what this book is all about.

First of all, by receiving His Spirit into our hearts, Christ wants to lift us to union with Himself. And then, through that union, He wants us to *follow the Spirit's leading, be cleansed by the Spirit, worship in the Spirit, abide in the Spirit,* and finally, *walk in the Spirit* so that others might see His reflection in us. Christ emptied Himself on that Cross so that we might not only come to Him, but also allow Him to reveal His glory through us to the world.[12]

---

9        Genesis 1:26; 1 Corinthians 11:7
10     Romans 3:23
11     Hebrews 2:6-8
12     Philippians 2:7; Romans 12:2

The object of the "church," then, is to be such a powerful reflection of Christ that the world not only would acknowledge the glory, which is God's, but also that it would want to personally possess that glory.

## A Perfect Example

Let me give you a great example.  There was a woman on our recent trip to Israel who was such a powerful reflection of Christ that not only did people acknowledge her life as totally supernatural, but you could see that many of them yearned to have just a small portion of the joy and enthusiasm that she possessed.

Christine suffers from a debilitating disease (which she was born with) that stunts her growth.  It's a form of child osteoporosis where the skeletal bones are unable to sustain weight.  They constantly fracture and break.  So, Christine is obviously very small (she is about 3 ft. tall) and permanently confined to a wheel chair.

But, no matter.  This incredible woman has been married for 25 years.  She has been a missionary in India and won several scholarships for her artwork (one to the Louver in Paris).  She scuba dives, para sails and is a gymnast who works out on the trampoline daily.  No self-pity here.  Just a striving to be all that God wants her to be!

When you talk to Christine, the light of Jesus absolutely exudes from her face. The joy of the Lord and His exuberance radiates from her. And, her enthusiasm is totally contagious. She truly is a living example of Christ. Others are not only drawn to her, they want what she has! Here is a beautiful woman who not only has been born of the Spirit, but she is also (metaphorically speaking) "walking in the Spirit."

Unfortunately, all too often just the opposite occurs. We're *born of the Spirit* (God's Spirit lives in our hearts), but we don't *walk in the Spirit*. Here's a tragic example.

## An Example: Born in the Spirit Only

I recently heard a story about a pastor named Bruce and his family. Bruce captivated his entire town. He was handsome, gregarious and everyone loved him. He had a beautiful wife, Janice, who was head of the women's ministry team at church, and four wonderful children. In the last four years, Bruce's church had grown from just over 300 to just under 3000. He was a fabulous preacher, knew the Scriptures backwards and forwards and kept everyone glued to his teachings. From the outside, everything looked great. Inside, however, it was another story.

Because of his excessive perfectionist tendencies and his insatiable desire to control, Pastor Bruce became almost intolerable to work with. His assistant pastor and his whole office staff were barely hanging on. They also knew about Bruce's adultery.

Against everyone's advice, and surely the nudging of the Holy Spirit, Bruce decided to privately counsel a newly divorced woman. By doing so, he quenched God's Spirit in him. Rather than heed to *His* leading, which is the mark of a spiritual Christian, he turned Him off.[13] And as the enemy would have it, that woman eventually became his lover. When Janice became aware of the affair, she and the children left Bruce and the whole church began to disintegrate. The community that once had been so enamored with Pastor Bruce, suffered a horrible blow; and of course, the opponents of Christ rejoiced. The witness of the Lord became completely defiled through Bruce.

This story is true, not only in our community, but in thousands of others across the United States. *Lifeline for Pastors* recently noted that about 800 pastors a month are now leaving the pulpit. Many of their stories are similar to the above.

Pastor Bruce's situation probably started out innocently enough. But slowly he began to follow his own feelings and desires *over* the leading of the Holy Spirit and what he knew God wanted him to do. One

---

[13]     Galatians 6:15; Romans 6:14

thing led to another and he ended up quenching God's Spirit and, operating solely in the flesh, out of his *own* wisdom and strength. In this condition, what image is he portraying? Christ's? I think not! Even though Christ still lives in his heart, the life that he reflected in his actions certainly was not Christ's, but his own. In other words, he "glorified himself." The tragic part of Bruce's story is not necessarily that his marriage and family fell apart, although that's pitiful; the sad part is that his actions portrayed a lie. He gave a false, erroneous, untrue, misleading and incorrect impression of Christ.

Think of Bruce's four kids. Two of them were teenagers when this story happened. Will they want what they saw in their dad's life? Again, I think not! In fact, all four kids have since left the church and it probably will be a long time before they are able to separate the real 'Life of Christ' and the life they saw their dad live. (Interestingly, again *Lifeline for Pastors* notes that 81% of adult children of pastors eventually have to seek professional help.)

## Another Example

I recently received a heart-wrenching letter from John, a delightful prisoner I have been corresponding with. He stated that his Dad was a preacher when he was growing up, but constantly abused him verbally, rejected every idea he had and showed him absolutely no love at all. As a result John transferred his feelings of resentment and bitterness towards God the Father. And of course, one thing led to another and he ended up committing the crime that landed him in prison.

Reconciling the loveless behavior of his father with the truth of how God really sees him has been the challenge of his life. He is just now learning how to break through the strongholds that were erected so many years ago as a result of his father's un-Christ like actions.

You have no idea how common the above stories are. And, you have no idea how many thousands have been turned off by the hypocrisy that these kind of stories portray. One woman said to me after her own pastor fell, "Well, if he as a pastor can't make it, I surely can't!"

*Our words and our life actions must match, otherwise we are no different than the secular world and it matters not that we say we are Christians.*

## The Scandal of the Evangelical Conscious

Ron Sider, a professor of Theology, Holistic Ministry and Public Policy at Eastern Baptist Theological Seminary, has written a book about this type of hypocrisy. It's called *The Scandal of the Evangelical Conscious*. Here are some of his comments:

"The heart of the matter is the scandalous failure to live what we preach. The tragedy is that poll after poll by Gallup and Varna show that evangelicals live just like the world. Contrast that with what the New Testament says about what happens when people come to living faith in Christ. There's supposed to be radical transformation in the power of the Holy Spirit. The disconnect between our Biblical beliefs and our practice is just heart-rending."

He continues, "I'm a deeply committed evangelical. I've been committed to evangelical beliefs and to renewing the evangelical church all my life. And the stats just break my heart. They make me weep. And somehow we must face that reality and change it.

"Evangelical Christians and born-again Christians get divorced just as often, if not a little more, than the general population. And Barna has discovered the 90% of the born-again Christians who are divorced got divorced *after* they accepted Christ...Several studies find that physical and sexual abuse in theologically conservative homes is about the same as elsewhere. [These] statistics show that they don't live what they're talking about. And sure, I'm afraid that's hypocrisy."

And he continues, "Cheap grace is right at the core of the problem. Cheap grace results when we reduce the gospel for forgiveness of sins only; when we limit salvation to personal fire insurance against hell; when we misunderstand persons as primarily souls; when we at best grasp only half of what the Bible says about sin; when we embrace the individualism and materialism and relativism of our current culture...Embracing Jesus means not just getting fire insurance so that one doesn't go to hell, but it means embracing Jesus as Lord as well as our Savior... Salvation means a new transformed life through the power of the Holy Spirit...It's a new, transformed lifestyle *that you see visibly in the body of believers*...Where people would say, 'Wow, what's going on here?'"

In other words, people would want what we have!

## A Few More Examples

I received a beautiful letter from a brother in the Lord who just lost his wife to cancer. Listen to his graphic description of modern day Christianity:

"I have been devouring the writings of many of the ministries of one to two hundred years ago. Christianity has now, in so many ways, become the loathsome and compromised thing that many of these writers warned of and feared. *The trite, self-help drivel that passes for Christian teaching these days is astonishing*...and at times infuriating.

"There are startling few these days who teach the glorious truth of the death and resurrection of Christ as the power that works in us moment by moment. What a wonderful path! What a precious Life is being wrought in us as we are brought to Glory!

"Many of the classical writers I have enjoyed are often derogatorily referred to today as mystics, like Andrew Murray, Oswald Chambers and even Spurgeon because they talk about matters of the exchanged life. *What could be more mystical than the very Son of God being manifested in our mortal flesh and our being conformed into His image?*" (R.F., Idaho)

———————

Another letter from a prisoner in Avenal State Prison articulates very much the same thing:

"The stagnant water that is a result of these joyless Christians is reflected in their life style that goes no further than words of the tongue. It's sad and it hurts me inside, but I can only minister to their hearts, in love and compassion, because I understand how it is to be in bondage to so many small vices that are like chains and as small as they are, they end up binding you totally.

"***Religion is no more than an occult to some and to others a light switch that they themselves switch on and off at their own convenience.***"

So we can begin to see that there's a big difference between just being "born anew in the Spirit" and experientially "walking in the Spirit," where we truly glorify and reflect Christ.

## What Does *Glorifying God* Mean?

As we begin, let's explore what the word "glorify" really means. In the Hebrew the word is *kabod* and in the Greek, it is *doxazo*. Interestingly enough, there are really two different aspects of this word:

1) To glorify means to shine, to demonstrate and to manifest the divine. (Exodus 16:7; 24:16) In other words, glory represents the Lord's presence. Throughout Biblical history, the glory of God was shown forth in the Pillar of cloud and fire that traveled with God's people and that rested on Mt. Sinai. (Exodus 24:15-18) That glory also filled the tabernacle in the wilderness. Listen to Exodus 40:34-35, "Then a cloud covered the tent of the congregation, and *the glory of the Lord filled the tabernacle.* And Moses was not able to enter into the tent of the congregation, because the cloud abode thereon, and *the glory of the Lord filled the Tabernacle.*" Often it would come at the hour of sacrifice. (See Leviticus 9: 6, 23). Solomon's temple was another anointed place where God's glory permanently dwelt. (See 1 Kings 8: 11; 2 Chronicles 7:1-3). God manifested Himself in the Shekinah Glory and was said to reside in the Holy of

Holies. His glory could be seen emanating from the temple for miles around. Also, God's glory could be seen through some of the Old Testament prophets' visions, through Stephen in the New Testament (Ezekiel 1:28; Isaiah 40:4-5; Acts 7:55) and through storms and other displays of God's character. (Psalms 19:1-6; 57:11; 96:3; Isaiah 2:10) And finally, God's glory is something we will *all* see when Christ returns (1 Peter 2:12) and we get to go to heaven. (1 Peter 1:11; 4:14-16; 5:10; Revelation 21:10-11)

2) To glorify can also mean to reflect, show forth, demonstrate and express the image of an object or person that it may be seen by all. *It means to add something to someone's character that in itself it does not have.* In the New Testament *doxazo* can mean to signify, extol and ascribe honor to. (John 11:4; 12:16, 23; 13:31; Matthew 5:16; 9:8; 15:31; Romans 15:6, 9; Galatians 1:24; 1 Peter 4:16) It is most often used of an *external manifestation.* According to the Bible, to glorify God means to bring Christ's innate glory or radiance to light, to manifest it or to reflect it. (John 17:1)

Glory, then, seems to be the vehicle that conveys and reveals the true presence of God. In Scripture, *glory means possession of the character, beauty and majesty that belong to the Lord. It means an exact representation of His being. It means reflecting His presence, His essence, His soul, His Life and His Name.* Thus, to glorify God is to manifest all that God is. It's showing forth *His Self,* not our own.[14] It's *His* glory brought to light in us.[15]

Hebrews 1:1-4 expresses it this way, "God, who at sundry times and in diverse manners spoke in time past unto the fathers by the prophets, hath in these last days spoken unto us by His Son, whom He hath appointed heir of all things, by whom also He made the worlds; Who, being *the brightness of His glory*, and *the express image of His person*, and upholding all things by the Word of His power, when He had by Himself purged our sins, sat down on the right hand of the Majesty on high."

## Jesus is Our Example

In the New Testament, the word *glory describes the revelation of the character, nature and presence of God in the Person of Christ.* (John 12:28) In truth, Jesus *is* God's glory. He *is* the manifestation of divine glory and He *is* the express image of God the Father.[16] He is the "King of Glory." Consider Psalm 24:7-10: "Lift up your heads, O ye gates; and be ye lifted up, ye everlasting doors; and the King of Glory shall come in. Who is this King of glory? The Lord strong and mighty, the Lord mighty in battle. Lift up your heads, O ye gates; even lift them up, ye everlasting doors; and the King of glory shall come in. Who is this King of glory? The Lord of hosts, He is the King of Glory."

---

[14]    John 14:13; 16:14
[15]    John 11:4; 17:1, 5
[16]    Hebrews 1:3; John 17:5; John 1:14; 2 Peter 1:17

How did Christ reflect the Father's glory? Well, first the glory of the Lord was present at His birth (Luke 2:9); then, at the beginning of His miracles (John 2:11); then in His ministry (John 12:37-41); at His transfiguration (Matthew 17:1-8); and finally, at His hour of passion. (John 12:23; Hebrews 2:9)

His resurrection and ascension are also seen as a manifestation of His Father's glory. (Luke 24:26; Acts 7:55; 1 Timothy 3:16; 1 Peter 1:21) What could possibly reveal the Father's glory more than Christ being raised from the dead? And when He returns again it will be with great power and glory. (Mark 13:26) Glorifying His Father and doing His will was the whole reason Christ came.

During Christ's lifetime, He manifested the Father's image perfectly; whether sharing the Father's Love to the Samaritan woman at the well; or His compassion to the children He taught; His godly exhortation to His disciples; or His rebuke to the Pharisees. *In whatever Christ did, He glorified the Father.*[17]

"For God, who commanded the light to shine out of darkness, hath shined in our hearts, to give the light of the knowledge of the glory of God in the face of Jesus Christ." (2 Corinthians 4:6)

---

[17]    John 17:1, 4-5; 13:31: 14:13

And this is the exact mission and purpose that Christ has for us. We are to glorify Him in all that we do. (John 15:8) "I will glorify Thy Name for evermore." (Psalm 86:12)

## Floodlight Ministry

J. I. Packer, again in his book, *Keep in Step with the Spirit*, relates a very interesting personal story:

"I remember walking to church one winter evening to preach on the words "He shall glorify Me," seeing the building floodlit as I turned a corner, and realizing that this was exactly the illustration my message needed. When floodlighting is well done, the floodlights are so placed that you do not see them; you are not in fact supposed to see where the light is coming from; what you are meant to see is just the building on which the floodlights are trained. The intended effect is to make it visible when otherwise it would not be seen for the darkness, and to maximize its dignity by throwing all its details into relief so that you see it properly. This perfectly illustrates the Spirit's new covenant role...

"Think of it this way. It is as if the Spirit stands behind us, throwing light over our shoulder, on Jesus, who stands facing us. The Spirit's message to us is *never* look at Me...but *always* look at Him and see His glory."

# God's Image

As we stated earlier, man was *originally* created in the image of God (Genesis 1:27), but after Adam and Eve fell because of sin, all mankind was subsequently born with a sin nature–*the image of Adam*, not God.

"And Adam lived an hundred and thirty years, and begot a son *in his own likeness, after his [own] image,* and called his name Seth." (Genesis 5:3) 1 Corinthians 15:49 also validates this, "And as we have borne the image of the earthy, we shall also bear the image of the heavenly."

The whole point of being "born anew in the Spirit" (John 3:3) is that we might once again receive God's Spirit (*positionally* become one with Him) so that through the sanctification process we can regain the image of God (*experientially* showing forth Christ-likeness). Then, the attributes of Christ's Love, patience, commitment, loyalty, self-denial, self-giving, obedience and joy may be seen through us. However (as we will see next chapter), it's only by our constant choice that we are able to "walk in the Spirit" reflecting His image in our every day lives. This doesn't happen automatically. Remember Pastor Bruce.

Our purpose for being called by God is to be continually filled with His Spirit. It is then that we can show forth His character and His Love (floodlight ministry), and not ourselves. We are to moment by moment relinquish ourselves so that Jesus' Life can flow through us and the Father can be glorified. This is sometimes called "the exchanged life." We give Him our life, and He gives us His. This is what allows us to be *living examples of Christ* (not just good talkers). (1 Corinthians 13)

Consequently, when God asks us to love Him with all our heart, mind and soul, what He is really asking is that we exchange our own image—all our own natural thoughts, emotions and desires that are usually contrary to His—for the Image that we were created to bear–<u>His</u> supernatural Love, Thoughts, and Power. As Romans 8: 29 tells us, we are predestined "to be conformed to the image of His Son."

## What's an Image?

An image is an exact likeness of something. It's a visible representation or reproduction of the form of a person. As we allow God to conform us more and more into *His* likeness, it will then be *His* image that we'll portray to the world, not our own.

The Bible tells us the chief duty of man is to glorify, reflect and show forth Christ in all we do. This is the chief aim of the Christian Life.[18] Now, worshiping God is important and it is the key to intimacy with Christ, as we will see later. But *worshiping God* is something we

---

[18]    Psalms 22:23; Matthew 5:16; Isaiah 24:15

do on the "inside," whereas *glorifying God* is something we show forth "externally." **Consequently, glory is the result of something that has already occurred on the inside.**

Glorifying God brings Christ's Love and attributes into prominence. It also manifests <u>His</u> plans and purposes for us.

## Self-Image

Unfortunately as we said before, glorifying God doesn't happen automatically. Just because we are born in the Spirit doesn't assure us of being able to walk in the Spirit. Just like experiencing His Love in our lives, the ability to glorify God involves a constant choice: to reflect His Life <u>or</u> to glorify self.[19]

Jeremiah 9:23-24 summarizes the choice that is always before us: "Let not the wise man glory in his wisdom, neither let the mighty man glory in his might, let not the rich man glory in his riches, but *let him that glorieth glory in this, that he understandeth and knoweth Me, that I am the Lord, which exercise loving-kindness, judgement, and righteousness, in the earth: for in these things I delight,* saith the Lord."

When we choose to adhere to and follow what *we* want, feel and think over what God has told us to do, like Pastor Bruce we'll quench His Spirit in us and thus

---

[19]     Psalms 115:1; John 8:54; Revelation 18:7; Romans 11:13

show forth our own image rather than His. (Psalm 81: 12) We must always keep in mind that our "self-image' will <u>never</u> bring anyone to the Lord, <u>never</u> restore any relationships and <u>never</u> heal any marriages. Remember, Jesus in John 5:31 warned us that, "If I bear witness of Myself, My witness is not true." Again, if Jesus says this about Himself, how much more it must be true of us! Only by reflecting and showing forth Christ's image will others truly be touched, changed and, want what we have.

Therefore, our purpose as Christians is to reflect the Lord, not ourselves. We must learn how to follow <u>His</u> Spirit, be cleansed by <u>His</u> Spirit, filled with <u>His</u> Spirit and then walk by <u>His</u> Spirit, so we can show forth <u>His</u> likeness to the world, not our own.

## Pride vs. Humility

Reflecting our own image to the world and not Christ's is really the definition of pride. It's putting ourselves and what we want, think and feel ahead of God and others. Pride is that choice we make to rely upon our own mental, physical and soulish self, not the Lord. The essence of pride is always self-centeredness and often develops when we exchange our intimate, *experiential* knowledge of God (gained through life experience) for *intellectual* knowledge of Him (head knowledge only).

The Bible tells us that *humility* is the opposite of pride. A humble Christian is one who is content to know the Lord from his heart, not his head. He readily recognizes, acknowledges and confesses his sin and self; thus he is able to be filled with the Spirit and reflect Christ in all He does. A humble person will <u>not</u> try to draw attention to himself but always to his Lord. Again, the floodlight ministry. Therefore, *the essence of humility is other-centeredness.*

On the other hand, a prideful Christian will covet all the attention he can get and do whatever he can to make a name for himself. No matter how many masks he has to put on and no matter what he must say or do, he's committed to maintaining his own notoriety and position. Thus, a proud person really has a very difficult time acknowledging his own faults. Consequently, he must continually keep up a facade, hide his insecurities and master his failures. A prideful Christian is also disappointed when someone else is praised or thanked or somehow gets the glory because he covets all the attention for himself.

I once read a very provocative statement about pride verses humility. I can't remember exactly where it's from, but it goes something like this: "If Christians are not growing into humility–constantly denying themselves and elevating Christ, then they will be swelling up in pride–parading their *own* image, gifts and anointing. There's no in between!"

Along this same line of thinking, something that has always puzzled me is how many so-called "great men of God" *on stage* are totally different people *off stage*. Chuck and I have had the privilege of knowing many such men and had the opportunity to see them in both situations. And I will tell you, it's a shock, because so many of these preachers' lives are a mess! Their <u>words</u> on stage and their <u>lives</u> off stage don't match at all. On stage, they spout Scriptures and speak about the importance of humility. But off stage they act like raving maniacs if they don't get their way. Something is desperately wrong! And it's always been a mystery to me as to how God can continue to use them.

But, Judson Cornwell, the late author of the book *Forbidden Glory*, gave me the answer to this. He says that "God's anointing is <u>not</u> to be taken as an approval of a lifestyle." In fact, Cornwell goes on to say that in the Old Testament, God even used a donkey to bring about His will. This explained a lot to me personally, but the sad truth is that this kind of hypocrisy causes many to stumble.

God's glory is something that doesn't belong to us. It's *God's* glory! And His purpose is that our lives reflect it. As Judson Cornwell puts it: "to bask in our own image or glory is forbidden."

It's called *pride.*

# God Hates Pride

The Bible tells us that "God hates pride." (Proverbs 16:5, 18)

The reason He hates pride so much is because pride separates us from God; it quenches His Spirit in us; and it prevents God's Life in our hearts from flowing out into our lives. Pride not only builds walls between God and ourselves, it also puts a barrier between others and us. It constantly brings contention, division and strife. Therefore Satan revels in the proud. He will do anything he can to get Christians to trade in their humility and intimate relationship with Christ for pride and intellectual knowledge of Him. He presses, pushes and drives for this because he knows these kind of prideful believers present a false image of what real Christianity is all about. And that, of course, is his real intent and motive–to divide and conquer.

Here are some interesting facts about pride:[20]

- Pride is an acid that turns the finest fruit bitter.
- Pride is a superficial weed that grows in all soils, without need of water or care.
  It consumes and destroys every living thing that it overshadows.
- Pride is a swelling of the heart filled with ego and self-importance.
- Pride raises us above others until we look down upon them.

---

[20]     www.discoverthebook.org/message

- Pride is a cancer that rots the soul. A man
    infected with pride needs nothing...
    not even God.
- Pride is the total inability to see
    beyond ourselves.
- Pride is spoken of leaven in Scripture because
    it corrupts by puffing up.

God exhorts us, "Let nothing be done through strife or vainglory, but in lowliness of mind *let each esteem other better than themselves*. (Philippians 2:3)

Scripture's perfect example is, of course, Jesus, whom Paul describes in Philippians 2:5-11:

"Let this mind be in you, which was also in Christ Jesus, who, being in the form of God, thought it not robbery to be equal with God; but made Himself of no reputation, and took upon Him the form of a servant, and was make in the likeness of men: And, being found in fashion as a man, *He humbled Himself,* and became obedient unto death, even the death of the cross. Wherefore, God also hath highly exalted Him, and given Him *a Name* which is above every name, that at the Name of Jesus every knee should bow, of things in heaven and things in earth, and things under the earth: and that every tongue should confess that Jesus Christ is the Lord, to the glory of God, the Father."

If anyone had a legitimate reason to be prideful, it would have been Christ. He was God's only beloved Son. Yet He, even He, humbled Himself and became obedient unto death. Humility, therefore, is the only pathway to genuinely reflecting Christ and being a living example of all that He is.

What is God's plan for our lives? To create in us the image of His Son through the process of humility so that we can reflect and glorify Him in all that we do. Like the floodlights that illuminate buildings, we need our actions to cause others to see Christ–nor only His reality but also their own personal need of Him.

# Chapter One Questions

1) What exactly happens at our new birth? (Acts 2: 38; Ezekiel 36:26; 1 John 5:12)

2) Does receiving His Spirit in our hearts guarantee our being able to "walk in the Spirit"? Why?/ Why not?

3) Christ wants to lift us to union with Him and through that union enable us to reflect His character. What are the five things we must learn in order to assure this?

4) What is God's purpose for teaching us how to "walk in the Spirit"? (Romans 12:2)

5) What then is the object of *the church* as a whole? Are we doing this?

6) The heart of the problem is that we have failed to live what we preach. Why has this occurred?

7) Define "glorifying God." (Hebrews 1:1-4)


8) Jesus is our perfect example to follow.  Why?
   (Philippians 2:7-9)


9) Name some of the specific events where the glory
   of God is revealed. (Luke 2:9; John 2:11;
   Matthew 17:1-8; John 12:23)


10) What, then, is our purpose for being called by
    God? (Romans 8:29; Psalm 22:23;
    Matthew 5:16;Isaiah 24:15)


11) What happens when we don't glorify God?
    Whose image do we portray then? (John5:31;
    Jeremiah 9:23-24)


12) Why does God hate pride so much?
    (Proverbs 16:5, 8)

# Warfare Prayer

Dearest Lord: I desire to be a "reflection of Your image," so that my family, friends and others will see You in me and want what I have. Therefore, I choose to give You anything in me that would prevent my hearing directly from Your Spirit. I present my body as a living sacrifice, holy and acceptable unto You, which is my reasonable service. And I choose *not* to be conformed to this world but to be transformed (into Your image) by the renewing of my mind, that I may prove what is Your good and acceptable and perfect will. (Romans 12:1-2)

I choose to *put on* the whole armor of God that I might be able to stand against the wiles of the enemy, having done all to stand strong. First of all, I choose to stand by having my loins girt about with truth, **wearing the breastplate of righteousness and Love guarding my heart**. (Ephesians 6:13-14; 1 Thessalonians 5:8)

# Chapter Two
## So, What's the Problem?

## The War

Being endowed with the image of God in our hearts does <u>not</u> guarantee our ability to manifest that image out in our lives. In other words, being "born anew" by His Spirit does <u>not</u> assure us of being able to "walk by" His Spirit. Why? Because there's a war going on in our souls. A huge war! A war between our *flesh* (our natural life in our soul) pulling us one-way and the Spirit of God (God's supernatural Life in our hearts) pulling us the other.

Paul warns us about this conflict in Romans Chapter 7 when he says: "For that which I do I allow not: for what I would, that do I not; but what I hate, that I do. If then, I do that which I would not, I consent unto the law that it is good." Paul goes on to explain, rather strongly, sins's power to derail us. "Now then it is no more I that do it, but sin that dwelleth in me. For I know that in me (that is, in my flesh,) dwelleth no good thing: for *to will* is present with me; but how to perform that which is good I find not." (verses 15-18) "I find then a law, that, when I would do good, evil is present with me." (Vs.21) *"But I see another law in my members, warring against the law of my mind, and bringing me into captivity to the law of sin which is in my members.  O wretched man that I am!  Who shall deliver me from the body of this death?"* (Vs.23-24)

Paul is saying here that we are unable to deliver ourselves from this conflict and if we were left this way, our soul would be in perpetual agony.  In other words, there is <u>not</u> the slightest chance of a peaceful co-existence between our flesh and our spirit.  Our soul simply does not want to be changed and it will fight to maintain its rights. Paul is saying here that we need a savior, a deliverer, a lifesaver—someone greater and wiser and smarter than us in order to set us free.  Paul goes on to answer his own question in verse 25, "who shall deliver me from the body of this death?"  Then, he says, "I thank God *through Jesus Christ our Lord that we can be set free*".  Paul is saying here that Jesus is our Deliverer, our Savior and the One who brings us life, liberty and acceptance.  And, because of <u>His</u> provision in sending us the indwelling Holy Spirit, we can, *if we so choose*, be set free.

*The next question is, how?  How does the Holy Spirit set us free?*

The answer (found again at the end of verse 25): *"So then with the <u>mind</u> I myself serve the law of God; but with the <u>flesh</u>, the law of sin."*

Here, again, Paul is describing the war that goes on within us and he is saying that the Mind of Christ is what the Holy Spirit will work through to set us free.

Consequently, recognizing the struggle between the *power of sin* that resides in our souls and bodies and the *Power of God* in our minds is of the utmost importance. If we don't understand this conflict or how to resolve it, we will succumb to the enemy every time and he will have a continual entrance into us.

Let's see if we can shed more light about this relentless war.

## Explanation of the Struggle

As Christians, there are two spiritual forces or entities struggling against each other inside of us. One is called: *the old self, the flesh* or *the old man* (Adamic nature); and the other is called: *the new self, the spirit* or *the new man* (God's Life in us). If we choose to follow *the old self*, we would be called a "carnal Christian" which means we have been born of the Spirit, but are <u>not</u> walking by or in Him. If on the other hand, we choose to follow *the new self*, we would be called a "spiritual Christian," one not only born again spiritually, but also one walking in the Spirit. *Amazingly, this struggle does not occur until after we become believers.* Up until that time, there is only *one* life in us–the old self (the old man or the old nature). It rules and reigns and that's it!

After our commitment to Christ and His Spirit coming to indwell us, however, there now are *two* natures in us–our old self and our new one. Consequently, *the rebirthing of our spirit by God makes absolutely no changes whatsoever in our "flesh."* It's still incurable. It's still fleshly and will *never* change on its own. Paul confirms this when he says, "in my flesh dwelleth no good thing." (Romans 7:18) Jesus also confirms this, "The flesh profits me nothing." (John 6:63) Consequently, as Christians, we're going to have to deal with the flesh until the resurrection.

The flesh is corrupt because it was created in the image of Adam, rather than the image of God. (Genesis 5:3). In other words, sin dwells in our flesh. Romans 7: 20-23 tells us that sin is a power that enslaves us. It's an energy force that dwells in our unregenerate bodies whose whole intent and purpose is to cause us to veer off course and to miss the mark–the mark being total conformity to the image of Christ. Satan uses this power of sin as his tool. And every time we choose to follow what our flesh is saying over what God is prompting us to do, we quench God's Spirit in us and become the enemy's pawns.

Pastor Bruce, from the last chapter, is a good example of this. He was overpowered, seized and carried off *by the flesh* like a prisoner of war. He was an unwilling captive, but wholly unable to rid himself of his bonds, his cords or bands of sin. He was like a traveler who was caught off guard by bandits that pounced on him and carried him off. What's so sad is how could such a holy man of God allow the bandits to creep up on him and capture him? How could someone who personally knew these Biblical truths, preached them and supposedly walked them, fall like this? If this can happen to a pastor, then what about us? Can we also get captured? You bet! Paul says that he, himself, continually experienced this battle.

"We are troubled on every side, yet not distressed; we are perplexed, but not in despair; Persecuted, but not forsaken; cast down, but not destroyed; *always bearing about in the body the dying of the Lord Jesus, that the life also of Jesus might be made manifest in our body.*" (2 Corinthians 4:8-10)

Paul knew the choices he had to make to continually free himself from the enemy in order that Christ's Life might show forth. We, too, must personally understand this perpetual struggle, as well as know the exact steps to overcome it.

## Characteristics of a Carnal Christian (Soulish Man)

Let's put all of this into language that we can understand. What are some of the characteristics that identify a "carnal Christian"? These are born-again Christians because they have the Spirit of God in them. However, because they have chosen to follow what the flesh has told them *over* God's promptings, their actions show forth self rather than God. Here are some further marks of identification:

Carnal Christians are often talkative and flippant, always making themselves the center of attention. (Reminds us of what we just read about pride.) They tend to use many words and look upon themselves as far more advanced than others. Consequently, they are often faultfinders. Working for the Lord is of the utmost importance to them, but they feel that everything must be done in a hurry. They do not wait on the Lord for His answers. They often rely upon their own personality and have a large spiritual vocabulary. They are ambitious and want to attain glory for themselves. They usually are uncommonly gifted, have great talent and magnetic personalities. But, again, they dwell on their own superiority.

The basic characteristics of the works of the flesh are independence or self-dependence, self-confidence and self-reliance. This Christian makes himself the center of attention and values self will above God's will. This person can do righteous deeds and do them well; however, as we have all seen, any good that the flesh does is an abomination in the sight of God and glorifies self.

Soulish believers try to satisfy their curiosity by studying prophecy. They believe that knowing mentally is the same thing as possessing experientially. They have great *acquired knowledge*, but not *Spirit revealed* knowledge. It's important to note, however, that increased spiritual head-knowledge will often strengthen our carnality, deceiving us into thinking we are spiritual.

The danger of the above is that because God's Spirit is suppressed, the soulish and bodily realm will rule, allowing the power of darkness to get an advantage. God designed the *sanctification process* to remove all hindrances so that the Holy Spirit can control us. **Sanctification is simply the process of restoring the image of Christ in us.** Unfortunately, many carnal Christians are unwilling to pay that price.[21] Thus, you can be born again by the Spirit and yet still spend 90% of your time in the soulish realm. If this is the case, your ministry and teaching will not produce any real life nor power. Listen to John 6:63, "It is the Spirit that quickeneth; the flesh profiteth nothing..."

Ask yourself, do any of the above characteristics describe you? If so, allow the Holy Spirit to personally reveal them to you and, in response, deal with them as God would have you *before* you get captured like Pastor Bruce.

Other "works of the flesh" are described in Galatians 5:19-21: "Now the works of the flesh are manifest, which are these: adultery, fornication, uncleanness, lasciviousness, idolatry, witchcraft, hatred, variance, emulations, wrath, strife, seditions, heresies, envyings, murders, drunkenness, revelings, and the like." Pastor Bruce would fall into this category.

---

[21] I am indebted to Watchmen Nee's book *The Spiritual Man* for much of this description.

# Characteristics of a Spiritual Christian (Spiritual Man)

Let's now describe a "spiritual Christian," one who not only has been born anew but who also is filled with the Spirit and walking by the Spirit, thereby glorifying the Lord.

This description is easy. Let's take a look at Galatians 5:22 and 1 Corinthians Chapter 13 for the characteristics that God sets down for these Christians.

Paul says that one walking by the Spirit is filled with all "the fruit of the Spirit"–love, joy, peace, long-suffering, gentleness, goodness, faith, meekness, temperance." (Galatians 5:22)

This description is then amplified in 1 Corinthians 13:4-8 where Paul says, "*Agape* suffereth long, and is kind; [His Love] envieth not; [His Love] vaunteth not itself, is not puffed up, doth not behave itself unseemly, seeketh not [its] own, is not easily provoked, thinketh no evil; rejoiceth not in iniquity, but rejoiceth in the truth; beareth all things, believeth all things, hopeth all things, endureth all things. [God's Love] never fails."

When I think of a spiritual Christian, there is one person in our ministry who always comes to mind. She is one who is willing to be a total servant to others. Nothing is too hard for her or beneath her. As I look around the Christian body, it's amazing to me how very few of these "servant heart" people there really are; Christians who are willing to scrub the toilet if necessary, work in the kitchen if needed or be *behind the scenes.* Humility again is the word that best describes a spiritual Christian. Most Christians, unfortunately, want to be *up in front* where they can be seen as "spiritual." They want the visible jobs! A Christian with a servant's heart is one who is only interested in what God thinks. And thus, they are willing to do whatever job is required. The Bible tells us that God's eyes are towards the humble, the unpretentious and the one who is free from pride.

Again, test yourself. Which of the above descriptions characterize you?

Remember a couple of things:

Whatever does not issue from depending upon the
    Spirit, is of the flesh.
Attempting to follow God without denying self is
    the root of all failure.
The flesh is Satan's workshop.
    Putting confidence in the flesh is death and
    will destroy our ability to glorify Christ.

Consequently, we must continually *judge ourselves* and constantly *bring our flesh into captivity* so that God's Life can come forth. Again, this is the *exchanged life* and what the sanctification process is all about.

# Where is the Battle Fought?

As we read at the beginning of this chapter, the war between the spirit and the flesh is usually waged in our minds. As Romans 8:6 expresses it:

"To be carnally minded is death; but to be spiritually minded is life and peace."

The word "minded" here is *phroneo*, which means an attitude, an outlook or a mental state. This Scripture is saying that if we follow what the flesh is telling us to do, then there will be a spiritual death that occurs. In other words, God's Spirit will be blocked, quenched and stopped in us and the resulting attitude will be fleshly. The only escape route is to have a willing attitude– constantly nailing the flesh to the cross and crucifying our own desires.

Romans 8:7 goes on to say that, "the carnal mind is enmity against God." It means that because the flesh is opposed to God, there is <u>not</u> the slightest chance of a peaceful co-existence. Now obviously, outward and blatant sins are hostile to God and we can all see and acknowledge that. But, *righteous acts can also be done independently of God and thus not considered of Him.* Anything done by or through the flesh does <u>not</u> please God. (Romans 8:8)

In fact, the better the flesh works, the farther away it is from God. For example, there are many "good" people who are simply unwilling to believe in the Lord Jesus Christ. If this is the case, all their good works and self-righteousness are of no avail and won't bring them any closer to God. In fact, these often become a stumbling block to ever really come to know Him. There are also many "good" Christians who still depend upon their own strengths to live a Godly life. The Bible says this is still going to produce "wood, hay and stubble"–worthlessness and meaninglessness in God's eyes! (1 Corinthians 3: 12)

The bottom line is simply "*those who are in the flesh* (no matter how good it seems) *cannot please God.*" This is the final verdict. Regardless of how good we are, how much we love others or how much we do for them, if these things are done in our own power and ability, they will <u>not</u> please God. Anything performed by the flesh, even though it may seem quite good, if it derives from *self* and not God's Spirit in us will not please Him. We may devise many ways to do good, to improve ourselves and to advance others, but if these ways come from carnal motives, it will not satisfy Him. *This is not only true of the unregenerate person; it is also true of a believer.* No matter how commendable or effective the works we do for the Lord, *if any of them are done in our own strength, through our own wisdom or by our own love,* we will fail the approval of God. God's pleasure or displeasure is <u>not</u> founded upon the principle of good and evil, but upon *what is the source of all these things.* Is it God's Spirit in us or is it self?

God looks at the motives of our heart, not just our actions. An action may be quite good and correct, yet the Lord always knows its true origin.

## The Dilemma

Why is it so hard to yield ourselves to the Spirit of God and allow His light, His presence and His glory to come forth? It's difficult because, as we have been saying, even though our "flesh" has been *positionally* crucified with Christ at our new birth, it's still <u>not</u> dead. It is very much alive and often revels with our help.

Paul confirms in Romans 6:6-7 that our old, evil heart-life (our old man) has been exterminated and done away with at our conversion; therefore, the power of sin's hold on the flesh has *positionally* been destroyed. As a result, we <u>can</u> (if we so choose) be set free from sin. *Christ in our new heart is now the overcoming power to constantly free us from this war.* This simply means that if we choose moment by moment to obey, trust, and follow God (*regardless of how we feel or what we think*), then we can, in His strength, overcome whatever the "flesh" is urging us to do and instead, be filled with His Spirit. This is called "putting off the old man" and "putting on the new" which we will discuss further in Chapter Five.

Ephesians 4:24 also exhorts us to "put on the new man, which after God is created in righteousness and true holiness." And Colossians 3:10 urges the same: "Put on the new man, which is renewed in knowledge after the image of Him that created him." Paul is referring to Christ's Life that resides in our hearts if we are born again and that we are daily to "put on" in our lives by faith. This becomes the new man, the new me.

Galatians 2:20 states, "I am crucified with Christ: nevertheless I live; yet not I, but Christ liveth in me: and the *life* which I now live in the flesh I live by the faith of the Son of God, Who loved me, and gave Himself for me."

What does it mean to "live by the faith of the Son of God"?

"Living by the faith of the Son of God," means to continually make a *faith choice* to allow Christ's Life from our hearts to come forth, regardless of our natural feelings or thoughts.

## Living by Faith

I can't talk about the subject of living by faith without expounding on the life and ministry of George Mueller, the famous teacher in the 1800's who by faith alone established an orphanage in England that fed and housed thousands upon thousands of orphans.

Mr. Mueller believed that faith rested upon the Word of God. He used to say, "When sight ceases, then faith has a chance to work." As long as there was any possibility of human success, he felt faith could accomplish nothing. Thus, his motto was "God is able to do this; I cannot."

His greatest desire was to live a public life of faith so that other's trust in God would be strengthened. He felt it would be living proof that faith works, if he, as a poor man, without asking the aid or finances of anyone, could simply by prayer and faith have all his needs met.

When there was no money, as happened often, he would simply say, "The Lord in His wisdom and love has not sent help, but I believe, in due time He will." He didn't know how God would do it, but he trusted He would! And, He always did! These are called *faith choices*. They are simply non-feeling choices to believe God in the midst of trials and testings.

As a result of George Mueller's life of prayer and faith, he was given the necessary money to build three orphanages, house and feed almost 2,000 children, buy all the furniture and supplies needed to furnish and run the homes and schools, and hire all the needed personnel to manage the facilities. Mueller expected God to answer and expected His blessings on his labor of love. And he always received it, because *he lived by faith*. Mr. Mueller epitomized Galatians 3:11, "The just shall live by faith."

What's so sad is that even as Christians, much of our faith rests upon what we can *see* and *feel*. God knows, however, that we can <u>never</u> truly live by faith as long as we are being manipulated by our senses. His Word reveals that the farther removed we get from our faith resting on the things that we see and feel, the more deeply we enter into a life of real faith in God.

Instilling naked faith is one of the reasons God allows "night seasons" in our lives. *When we are no longer able to "see," we will be forced to live by faith.* And when our faith finally stops being dependent on the realm of our senses, we will be free to enter into the *"rest of God."* God knows that the less we "see," the more faith we'll have to live by. In Jesus' words, "...blessed are they that have not seen, and yet have believed." (John 20:29)

## Our Choice is the Key

Let me explain. Every true believer who has given himself to the Lord has the Holy Spirit dwelling within him. His Spirit has united with our spirit and we have become born anew. Thus, we have Christ's power and His authority to crucify the flesh and have victory over Satan and sin. The problem is, as we will see in the next chapter, God has created us with a *free will*. In other words, we have the freedom to choose *whomever we want* to follow. And this, unfortunately, is not just a one-time choice, it's a choice that we will have to make every day, every hour of every day and every moment of every day!

Scripture tells us that we become a servant to whomever we choose to follow. (Romans 6:16-22) The evidence of whom we choose to serve will be manifested in our actions. The fruit from our lives will either reflect Christ or show forth self.

When we choose to follow the Lord, our lives will be filled with the fruit of His Love, joy and peace. Even though we may still face many trials, that strength of faith, that peace of mind and that Love of God will still be there. If on the other hand, we choose to follow what we think, feel and desire and make self-centered, fleshly choices, we'll open ourselves up to oppression by the enemy and lose our peace and our joy. That will be evident to all around us. Even though on the outside it might look like our lives are running smoothly, the "fruit" we exhibit will be the tell-tale proof to whom we have relinquished our lives and whose servant we have become.

In light of these things, where do we start with the transformation process? How do we "put off" the flesh and "put on" Christ? What do we do first? How do we overcome the flesh?

## Overcoming the Flesh

Ever since becoming a Christian, I have been fascinated with the words *overcoming* and *overcomers*. Listen to what Chapter 2 and 3 of Revelation promise those who overcome: "I will give [him] to eat of the hidden manna, and will give him a white stone, and in the stone a new name written, which no man knoweth saving he that receiveth it." (2:17); "I will give [him] power over the nations; and he shall rule them with a rod of iron...and I will give him the morning star." (2:26-28); "[he will] be clothed in white raiment; and I will not blot out his name out of the book of life, but I will confess his name before my Father, and before His angels." (3:5); "I will make a pillar in the temple of my God, and he shall go no more out: and I will write upon him the Name of my God, and the name of the city of my God, which is new Jerusalem, which cometh down out of heaven from my God; and *I will write upon him My new Name.*" (3:12)

And the most incredible promises of all, Revelation 3:21: "To him that overcometh will I grant to sit with Me in My throne, even as I also overcame, and am set down with My Father in His throne." And Revelation 21:7, "He shall inherit *all* things and I will be His God and he shall be My son."

Phenomenal Scriptures and promises!

"Overcoming" simply means relinquishing our fleshly self so we can be controlled by God's Spirit. 1 John 5:4 affirms this: "For whatsoever is born of God overcometh the world, even our faith. Who is he that overcometh the world, but he that believeth [is committed to, relies upon, trusts in] that Jesus is the Son of God."

And because we believe, trust and rely upon Him, we are committed to following the leading of His Spirit and obeying His commands. He tells us to "take every thought captive" and make the appropriate choices to *put off* our sin and self and *put on* Christ. (2 Corinthians 10:50; Ephesians 4:22-24)  In Chapter Five we'll be discussing the actual steps to doing this.  But before we get into those specifics, there are *three important concepts* we need to understand so that we *can be* overcomers and build a solid foundation:

## Three Important Steps to Overcoming

1) First, we must recognize there is a spiritual battle going on within us between the flesh and the Spirit and we are both the target and the prize.  It's critical that we see we are pawns in a much larger scheme of things and we can never let our guard down.

2) Next, we must know that God unconditionally loves us.  We must know this not only in our heads, but also in our every day experience.

3) And finally, in response to God's unconditional Love, we must learn what it means to love Him (to totally give ourselves over to Him) which includes learning: how to choose to follow His Spirit; how to be cleansed by His Spirit; how to worship in the Spirit; how to abide in the Spirit; and, how to walk by the Spirit.

# A Beautiful Example

Erica is a precious, young woman who works here at *The King's High Way* ministry. I asked her to write her story as she is one who has experienced first hand *the spiritual battle* that is raging around each of us; the importance of *knowing that God loves her*; and, in response to that Love, knowing how to *totally lay her life down* to the Lord so that He can use her. Erica is 29 years old. Here's what she had to say:

"As I write down my testimony, all that I can think about is *how far God has brought me.* It's nothing short of a miracle. I know I had to endure some of the bad stuff so that I could see the faithfulness and the goodness of God, and see that I was living in complete darkness–Satan's world.

I was an alcoholic and drug addict for ten years. I lived for it. It was who I was and my life. I was born into the dysfunctional lifestyle. I was so empty and lonely that I tried to end my life many, many times. I've been in jails, mental wards, four treatment centers (for a total of one and a half years), gone to Narcotics Anonymous, Alcoholics Anonymous and contracted Hepatitis C through I.V. drug use. Nothing I did, no matter what I tried, worked! Until I was on my way to the State Mental Hospital for 6 months court-ordered by the Judge. That's when the Lord found me and began to change my life. I finally surrendered!

The Lord has taken my old emotional outbursts and replaced them with a supernatural Love in my heart for others. Before, I didn't care who I hurt or used. Bitterness, hate and resentment consumed me.

God has healed me because He loves me! He has healed me from hepatitis C (it will be 2 full years this summer), from alcohol, from drugs, from cigarettes, from depression, from suicidal thoughts and abuses of all different kinds. If you would have told me that "God loved me" before, I would have told you, "you are nuts." Yet, after everything I did, He still loves me. I know it in my heart, it's not a head thing anymore. His faithfulness and Love are too evident. I can't deny this. It takes away all the pain and loneliness I experienced.

Because of His unconditional Love, God is showing me how to surrender my life back to Him. He is continually teaching me how to be a godly wife and mother. This has been a struggle, but I am learning that *my* ways don't work any more. I can't fix or change my family. In fact, I only seem to make things worse. The Lord is showing me that *He* can handle it all! Thus, I lay my husband, Bill, and my children down to the Lord every day and when I do, I see the hand of God move in such a visible way. It's absolutely amazing.

I love my husband and am learning so much through him. When I surrender my life to the Lord on a moment-by-moment basis, I'm able to love Bill with God's Love and he, in turn, can see Jesus in me. I know my husband and my children belong to the Lord and are simply a gift to me for which I thank the Lord everyday.

What I strive for now, is to be a *clean* vessel so that God can continue to use me."

It's important to understand that we can <u>never</u> overcome the flesh by "fleshly" means. In fact, we can <u>never</u> yield to the flesh at all! We cannot repair it, discipline it or educate it. The flesh must be crucified. Only by putting our sin and self at the Cross can we ever be liberated to live by the Spirit.

## Knowing God Loves Us

Thus, in order to be an overcomer like Erica, we must not only recognize the spiritual battle going on around us, we must also experientially learn that *God loves us*. God's Love is a gift that we all receive when we are born anew by His Spirit. Therefore, if we have asked Jesus into our heart to be our Savior, then not only has Jesus come into our heart, but His Love is there also. 1 John 4:8 tells us that "God is Love." And in John 17:26, Jesus tells us: "And I have declared...that the Love wherewith Thou hast loved Me may be in them, and I in them."

Saying that "we must know that God loves us" might sound a little simplistic, but let me tell you, it's one of the most important concepts to learn. Everything else hinges upon this one principle. Knowing God loves us is the *foundation* of our walk with Him. Again, this sounds so child-like, but in reality it's probably one of the most difficult things to really experience, especially if there are "strongholds" in our soul.

In our haste to be "like Jesus," many of us have forgotten this first basic step–to personally know the extent and the depth of God's Love. If we really knew how much He loved us, we would never fear what He might allow into our lives or doubt His power to cast out the imposters. We would always have the confidence and the trust to continually abandon ourselves into His care and know that He will take care of us no matter what. What happens if we don't know that we are loved by the Father, is that we won't have the confidence or the trust to lay our wills and our lives down to Him and <u>do</u> as He asks.

When I first began teaching about "faith choices" in the study *The Way of Agape,* my focus was on the two great commandments: "Thou shalt love the Lord thy God with all thy heart, and with all thy soul, and with all thy mind...and thou shalt love thy neighbour as thyself." (Matthew 22:37-39)

But after several years of hearing the reactions of the women in those first classes, I realized that there is *no way* that they could learn to surrender themselves completely to God and love others until they *first* personally knew that God loved them. Knowing that God loves us is the *foundation* of our faith walk. Without first being able to personally experience His Love and acceptance in our own lives, we're <u>never</u> going to be able to move forward in our Christian life.

Put it this way: it's impossible to lay our lives down to someone if we don't really think that person loves us. This principle is true no matter how long we have been Christians, no matter how many people we have led to the Lord, no matter how many Scriptures we know or how many Bible studies we have taught. If we really know that God loves us, then we'll have the confidence and the trust to continually relinquish our wills and our lives to Him and, thus, see His handprint of Love at every turn. This is what gives us the confidence to make choices we don't feel, because we know He'll be faithful to align our feelings with that choice and perform His will through us.

As Isaiah 49:16 so beautifully says, "Behold, I have graven thee upon the palms of My hands; *thy walls* are continually before Me."

If, however, we doubt His Love, we won't have the confidence to surrender ourselves, which will not only limit our ability to experience His personal touch on our own lives, but also hinder our passing along His Love to others. This doesn't mean that God isn't in our hearts, loving us. He is! It just means that because we have quenched His Spirit by doubt, we won't have that daily, living, experience of encountering His handprint at every turn. And if we're not sure of His Love, our feelings will continually scream, "It's scary. I can't do it. I'm afraid. It's going to fall flat! It won't work! I'm not sure! I can't."

Therefore, knowing God loves us personally is critical. It's a very important step to putting off the flesh, fighting the enemy and learning how to glorify God.

(If you have trouble believing that God loves you and will be faithful to perform what He has promised to you, I strongly suggest getting *The Way of Agape* textbook and specifically reading Chapter Seven, "How Do I Know God Loves Me?" You might also go over the *Knowing God Loves* Me Scriptures in the Appendix of that book and, by faith, choose to believe what God says in those Scriptures.)

Isaiah 43:2-5 reassures us: "When thou passest through the waters [trouble], I will be with thee; and through the rivers, they shall not overflow thee; when thou walkest through the fire, thou shalt not be burned; neither shall the flame kindle upon thee. For I am the Lord thy God...[You are] precious in My sight and...I have loved thee."

## Learning to Love God

The third concept in the process of becoming "overcomers" is learning how to really love God. Again, this sounds so easy and so simple and most of you would probably say, "But, I already love Him! What's to learn?" Well, loving God the way Scripture tells us is <u>not</u> easy, nor is it simple and most of us are <u>not</u> doing it!

The Greek word for "love," used in both of the great commandments, is the verb *agapao*. (Matthew 22:37-39) *Agapao* means "to totally give ourselves over to something," to be totally consumed with it or to be totally committed to it. In other words, what we *agapao* is what we willingly submit our wills and our lives to. It's what we put first in our lives. All our intentions and abilities are focused and consumed with this one thing.

Loving God entails *making faith choices to follow Him* no matter how we feel or what we think. It means "taking every thought captive," letting His Spirit cleanse us and renew our minds. It means *knowing how to worship Him* so that His Spirit can direct us and give us His insights. It means *knowing how to abide in His Spirit* so we can produce fruit in our lives. And loving Him means *knowing how to walk by His Spirit reflecting Him* in all we do. Of course, most of us already think we're loving Him. But if I asked you if you are doing *all of* the above things, how would you answer?

Learning to love God the way He desires is <u>not</u> an emotional love but a total commitment love.

## An Example: Unconditional Love

Steve was a young man with a nine-year-old daughter, Heather, whom he loved more than life itself. Steve had, however, a very difficult marriage, but he wouldn't consider leaving his wife because he adored Heather. Finally, his wife ended up filing for divorce and a bitter custody battle ensued. In order to manipulate her daughter's affections and possibly the court, Steve's ex-wife lied to Heather and told her horrible, mean and untrue things about her dad.

Shortly after that, Steve received the most hurtful, hateful and bitter letter from Heather that he could ever imagine. It absolutely devastated him because she accused him of all the lies her mom had told her, none of which were true. Steve crashed and burned for several days trying to decide how to defend himself and answer her accusatory letter. He envisioned writing a sharp letter back to Heather taking each point and blasting his ex-wife "out of the water" with the truth. He had the letter all written in his head, which would have finally put her in her place. He certainly would have been justified by the world's standards to do so.

But, since Steve loved the Lord more than anything else in the world, his conscience wouldn't let him write a letter like that. In fact, after several days the Holy

Spirit convinced Steve to write a godly letter to Heather telling her that if she wanted to, she could say mean things about him and even call him names if she liked, but that he would always unconditionally love her. Rather than pointing fingers at his wife, he asked Heather for her forgiveness for all the pain the situation had caused her.

After a few days, he received another letter from Heather. Only this time she said, "Daddy, I do forgive you and I do love you more than anything." At the custody hearing, Heather sat next to her dad and they talked together the whole time. The judge was impressed with the love the two obviously shared, and because of that he ruled in favor of Steve.

Truly, obeying and loving the Lord always pays off in the end! We *do* reap what we sow, either for good or for evil.

Could you have done what Steve did?

Loving God means totally giving ourselves over to Him and submitting our wills and our lives to Him in everything.

## *Agapao* vs. *Agape*

As we study the Greek <u>verb</u> *agapao*, it's important that we not get it mixed up with the <u>noun</u> *Agape* because they mean two totally different things.

The noun *Agape* means God's pure unconditional Love and it's always used as such in the Bible. The definition of *Agape* is found in 1 Corinthians 13:4-8 (see Chapter 2). Throughout Scripture, there is <u>never</u> a negative usage of the noun *Agape*. In fact, the word *Agape* was actually coined uniquely for its usage in Scripture, whereas the verb *agapao* means whatever we totally give ourselves over to. But, as we have just seen in the description of *the carnal Christian*, we can give ourselves over to something that is "good" (like God or caring for others), or we can give ourselves over to something that is worthless (like things of the world— money, materialism, pleasure, fornication, etc.).

Look at the following Scriptures and see some of the carnal things that people in the Bible "gave themselves over to":

John 3:19, "men loved [*agapao*] darkness rather than light, because their deeds were evil."

John 12:43, "For they loved [*agapao*] the praise of men more than the praise of God."

Luke 11:43, "Woe unto you, Pharisees! for ye love [*agapao*] the uppermost seats in the synagogues."

2 Timothy 4:10, "For Demas hath forsaken me, having loved [*agapao*] this present world."

1 John 2:15, "Love [*agapao*] not the world, neither the things that are in the world."

And lastly, Luke 6:32, "for sinners also love [*agapao*] those that love them."

Some current examples of things we agapao are careers, houses, money, pleasure and *self.*

This perhaps explains why so many Christian marriages are not working as God desires. Jesus tells us that the husband must love (*agapao*) his wife as himself and the wife is to revere her husband. Well, if the man is <u>not</u> truly loving God (submitting his will and his life to Him) as he should, then there's no way he can love his wife as himself. Nor will she be able to respond in reverence, as God desires. If the chain of command is not working properly, the whole process falls apart! (Note: This does not mean that the innocent party is "off the hook." God says we are even to love–agapao–our enemies.) To love each other as God desires means to lose ourselves (set ourselves aside), so that we can put the other's needs before our own. How many marriages are working like this?

## To Love God Means to Lose Self

So, to love God is <u>not</u> an emotional feeling. To love God means to surrender, relinquish and set aside our self-life and make a faith choice so that His Life can come forth from our hearts. Again, we'll discuss the practical steps of doing this in the upcoming chapters.

A Scripture that sums up what loving God means is Matthew 16:24. "If any man will come after Me, let him *deny himself,* and *take up his cross*, and *follow Me.*"

Because of our ignorance of the different types of natural, human love, as Christians we often get our feeling and emotional love (*storge*) confused and mixed up with this "commitment love" (*agapao*). And, because most of us have great emotional love for God, we think we are loving Him as He desires when, in fact, we are not even close.

Ever since I was a little girl, I have loved God. But my love for Him always seemed to fluctuate depending upon how I felt, how the other person was reacting and what my circumstances were. I see now that my early love for God was really an emotional love (*storge*) and not a commitment love (*agapao*) at all. And, the more I grow in learning to love God His way, the more I understand that affection love comes and goes, depending upon how we feel, what we think, and what our circumstances are. In other words, one day we're "up" and feeling *close* to God; the next day, because we feel awful, our circumstances are bad and others are treating us poorly, we feel *far* away from Him.

God clarifies this for us in Isaiah 29:13: "This people draw near Me with their mouths, and with their lips do honour Me, but have removed their heart far from me, and their fear [love] toward Me is taught by the precept of men."

## Do You Love God?

If I asked you, "Do you love God?" Most of you would automatically say, "Yes, of course I do!" But if you are really honest with yourselves, how often do you seek to put *His* will and *His* desires above your own? How often are you consumed with what *He* desires for your life and not what you want out of life?

*Can you honestly say that you desire God's will above your own happiness?*

This question puts it right into perspective, doesn't it? People everywhere are seeking happiness and contentment as their ultimate goal. Is this your goal? Or is it to set yourself aside and please God?

There was a woman in one of my classes who really took offense at my statement that we should desire God's will above our own happiness. She came to me afterwards and said, "Nancy, surely you mean our perception of happiness?"

I said, "No, I really believe there are many times when we must choose to do God's will over what we *know* will bring us happiness." There have been many times in my own life where I've had to make choices I knew would <u>not</u> bring me momentary happiness. And yet, I knew that in the long run nothing would compare with the joy I would experience as a result of choosing God's way over my own.

It's as if God is testing us. When difficult situations arise and the other person involved is obviously sinning, God is not only interested in their reactions, He is also watching ours. Humanly, we want to retaliate. And, even though we might be justified by the world's standards to do so, God's watching to see what we will do. Will we react immediately out of the flesh and end up spiraling downward into the pit, or will we catch ourselves and choose by faith (because we surely don't feel like it) to surrender our flesh and continue to walk by the Spirit? The wonderful part of this last scenario is that *after* we have dealt with our own fleshly emotions, the Lord will align our emotions with our faith choices and the result will be miraculous.

So, what then, is the problem? Why can't we all just automatically reflect Christ and His Life if we are believers? We're unable to do this because of three things: 1) There's a spiritual battle waging in our souls between the Spirit of God and the flesh and we often succumb to following the wrong one; 2) we're unable to reflect Christ in our lives because we don't really know that God loves us. Consequently, we don't trust Him enough to surrender our lives to Him; 3) as a result, we're unable to love Him–unable to totally give ourselves over to Him–and thus, unable to be overcomers and show forth His Life. Without understanding these three basic concepts, we'll *never* be able to build a foundation in our efforts towards reflecting Him in all we do.

# Chapter Two Questions

1) So what *is* the problem? Why don't we all, if we are Christians, automatically "walk by the Spirit" and show forth His image? (Romans 7:15-21)

2) Can't we deliver ourselves from this dilemma? (Romans 7:23-25)

3) Before we were born again, did we experience this struggle? Why?/ Why not?

4) When we were born again, we received a new heart and a new spirit, but what happened to our soul? Were there any changes there? Explain. (Romans 7:18; John 6:63)

5) What is sin? (Romans 14:23b)

6) List some of the characteristics of a carnal Christian. Now list a few of the characteristics of a spiritual Christian. Which do you see yourself as?

7) Where specifically is the battle between our flesh and our spirit fought? (Romans 7:23 & 25; 8:6-7)

8) Why is it so hard to follow the Spirit? (Romans 7:18, 21,23)

9) What does God exhort us to do with the "flesh"? (Ephesians 4:22-23; Colossians 3:8-9)

10) Why is our choice the *key* to our Christian walk?

11) What are the three steps to "overcoming" the flesh? (Ephesians 6:12; John 3:16; Matthew 22:37)

12) Why is it so important to know that God loves us and what does it mean to love Him in return? (John 17:26; Matthew 16:24)

13) What is the difference between the noun *Agape* and the verb *agapao*? (1 Corinthians 13:4-8; John 3:16)

# Warfare Prayer

Dearest Lord: I desire to be a reflection of Your image so that my family, friends and others will see You in me and want what I have. Therefore, I choose to give You anything in me that would prevent my hearing directly from Your Spirit. I present my body as a living sacrifice, holy, acceptable unto You, which is my reasonable service. And I choose *not* to be conformed to this world but to be transformed (into Your image) by the renewing of my mind, that I may prove what is Your good, acceptable and perfect will. (Romans 12:1-2)

I choose to "put on" the whole armor of God that I might be able to stand against the wiles of the enemy, having done all to stand strong. First of all, I choose to stand by having my loins girt about with truth and having on the breastplate of righteousness and Love guarding my heart. ***Next, I choose to shod my feet with the preparation of the Gospel of peace.*** (Ephesians 6:13-15)

# Chapter Three
## A Visual Picture of the Problem

Let's see if we can create a visual picture of the continual war that goes on in Christians between the power of God in our hearts and the power of sin that resides in our souls. Let's see what it looks like to be a *spiritual Christian* walking by the Spirit verses a *carnal Christian* choosing to follow the flesh.

If you have read any of my other books, you'll remember that I go into great detail comparing the internal architecture of our bodies to the floor plan of Solomon's Temple in the Old Testament. The parallel is phenomenal! Now, the reason I refer to Solomon's Temple rather than Herod's or the others is because Solomon's Temple was very special and very unique for three reasons:

1) It was the only Temple in which all the detailed plans—not only of the construction of the Temple, but also of all the furniture—were given to David by the Spirit of God. Listen to 1 Chronicles 28:11-12: "Then David gave to Solomon his son the *pattern* of the porch, and of its houses thereof, and of the treasuries thereof, and of the upper chambers thereof, and of the inner parlours thereof, and of the place of the mercy seat; and *the pattern*

*of all that he had by the Spirit,* of the courts of the house of the Lord, and all the chambers round about, of the treasuries of the house of God, and of the treasuries of the dedicated things."

*Pattern* in the Hebrew means "a copy of the original; a miniature model." No other Temple could boast of this *supernatural design*. Scripture tells us that Solomon's Temple was built specifically to glorify God. That was its purpose.

2) Also, Solomon's Temple was the only temple in which the Ark of the covenant rested.

3) And finally, it was the only temple in which the Shekinah Glory (God's Spirit) dwelt for 400 years, until the temple was destroyed.

We don't have a lot of time to go into great detail in this book because we have a more important mission to accomplish: how we glorify God. However before we proceed further, we do need to cover a couple of important points about the temple that I believe will help paint a visual picture for us.

As we said, Solomon's Temple was built specifically to glorify God. It was the place where God met with His creation, and the place where He dwelt. The Greek word for temple is *naos, which* means to dwell in or to inhabit. Scripture tells us that this temple was built to show that

God dwelt there and to manifest His glory and presence. For 400 years it stood on the top of Mount Moriah, in the middle of Jerusalem, with the Shekinah Glory (the sign of God's presence) emanating out from every portal. It was said that the windows in the Sanctuary were constructed wider on the inside and narrower on the outside, in order to capture the supernatural Light and funnel it outward. Can you just imagine what it must have been like? If you lived in Jerusalem or the nearby areas, you would have been able to look up to Mt. Moriah and see God's supernatural Glory exuding from every temple window and doorway. It reminds me of 1 Kings 8:10-11 which speaks of the priests not being able to minister because the glory of the Lord had so filled the house. Picture what the Israelites must have felt when they witnessed this!

**CHART 1:** This is a picture of the *outside* of Solomon's Temple and what it might have looked like when the Shekinah Glory came forth.

**CHART 2:** This is a picture of the *inside* or the floor plan of Solomon's Temple filled with God's Spirit.

You can see how God's Spirit emanated out from the Holy of Holies where He dwelt, through the Holy Place and Porch of the sanctuary, past the two bronze pillars to the Inner Court and on to the Outer Court.

Chart 1     **Shekinah Glory Shining Forth**

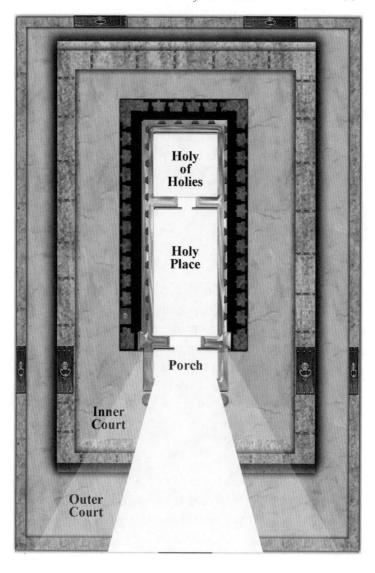

Chart 2 **Spirit Filled Temple**

# Human Temples

The New Testament tells us that the Shekinah Glory or God's presence now dwells in "temples made without hands." (Acts 17:24) Namely us! Several times the New Testament declares that *we*, as believers, are a temple of God and that the Lord wants to glorify Himself through us, as He did through Solomon's Temple.
(See **CHART 2**)

Several Scriptures in Corinthians validate this:
1 Corinthians 3:16, "Know ye not that ye are the temple of God, and that the Spirit of God dwelleth in you?" And 1 Corinthians 6:19-20, "What? Know ye not that your body is the temple of the Holy Ghost which is in you, which ye have of God, and ye are not your own? For ye are bought with a price: *therefore glorify God in your body, and in your spirit, which are God's.*" Finally 2 Corinthians 6:16, "For ye are the temple of the living God; as God hath said, I will dwell in them, and walk in them; and I will be their God, and they shall be My people." Jesus even refers in Mark 14:58 to His own Body as a temple.[22]

The Bible is making an analogy or a comparison in these Scriptures by saying that *as Christians* our body is a temple and that temple is now the dwelling place of the Holy Spirit.

---

[22]       For further references, see Acts 17:24 "priests unto God";
1 Peter 2:9; Revelation 1:6; 5:10

# The Temple of God

Let's now take a look at Solomon's Temple as a model or a blueprint of a New Testament believer. One who has the Spirit of God dwelling in him.

### CHART 3: The Floor Plan

First, note that the three main rooms of the sanctuary–the Holy of Holies, the Holy Place and the Golden Vestibule (or Porch)–were all made of *gold*. Even the furniture in these three rooms were solid gold. This will become very important later.

Just outside the Porch, note the change of metals from gold to bronze. Beginning with the two bronze Pillars, everything in the Inner Court–all the furniture–was *bronze*.

Surrounding the main sanctuary, note the *wooden*, hidden chambers that were supposed to be used by the priests to store the worship items for the Holy Place. However, it was here that the priests often stored their own personal idolatrous worship items, thinking that since they were out of sight, no one would see; no one would know. (Be sure to read Ezekiel 8:6-12.)

The gold symbolizes purity and holiness. The wood symbolizes humanity, our human nature or the flesh. And, the bronze symbolizes judgment–i.e., sin is still present.

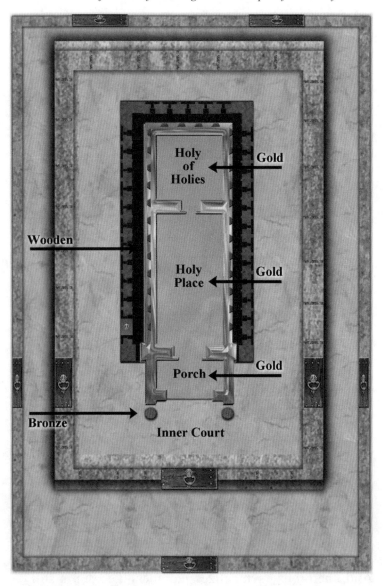

Chart 3

Again, this will become significant later.

## CHART 4: The Spiritual View

Let's now compare the different rooms of Solomon's Temple to the various parts of our own makeup and see if there are any parallels. I believe the Holy of Holies represents a believer's new spirit (*pneuma*); the Holy Place represents his new heart (*kardia*); the Porch or Golden Vestibule represents his new willpower or volition (*dianoia*). Remember, all three of these areas were fashioned in gold.

The Inner Court represents the conscious part of a man's soul–his natural will, natural thoughts and natural emotions; the secret, hidden, wooden chambers around the main sanctuary represent the hidden part of a believer's soul (*cheder*), the place where we store our hurts, doubts, and fears, thinking (like the priests) that because they are hidden *no one will see; no one will know.*

The Outer Court then represents a believer's body. When we speak of the "flesh," we mean both the soul (both the hidden part and the conscious part) and the body.

As a born-again believer, the **Spirit** that now dwells at the core of our being is not our "old" human spirit anymore, but a totally *new spirit* given to us at our new birth. That's what being "born again" actually means. (1

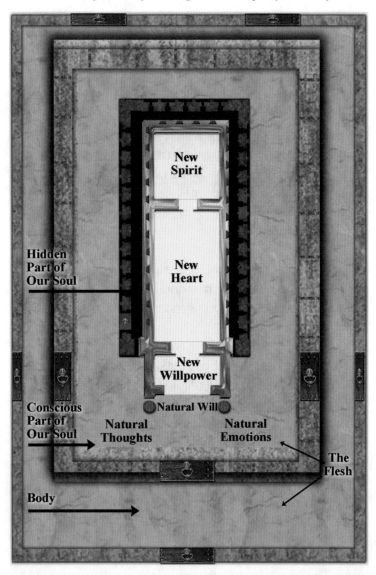

Chart 4

Peter 1:3, 23)  It means God's Spirit has united with our human spirit and we now have a *totally new Life source* or Power source.  The Spirits job is to regenerate, sanctify, assure, equip and empower us.

Our **heart**, then, is the place where "God's Life" is now brought into *new* existence by God's Spirit. Remember Ezekiel 36:26-27 which says, "A *new heart* also will I give you, and a *new spirit* will I put within you: and I will take away the stony heart out of your flesh, and I will give you a heart of flesh." (Ezekial11:19)

This new "heart of flesh" is Jesus' Life in us.  In other words, at our new birth God replaces our old heart life (our old, natural love and thoughts) with His brand-new heart life: His supernatural Love (*Agape)*, His supernatural Thoughts (*Logos*) and His supernatural Power (*Dunamis*).  (Romans 5:5; Hebrews 8:10)

So our old heart, which Scripture tells us is evil and incurable and unknowable from birth, (see Jeremiah 17: 9) *is totally replaced by a brand-new heart when we are born again by God's Spirit.*  Consequently, the Life that is now in our hearts is totally pure, totally incorruptible, and completely holy because it's Jesus' Life and not our own. This again is "Christ in [us], the hope of glory." (Colossians 1:27)

Therefore, as Christians, it's <u>not</u> our hearts that need to be transformed anymore; that was done at our new birth. It's *our lives or our souls* that are in such desperate

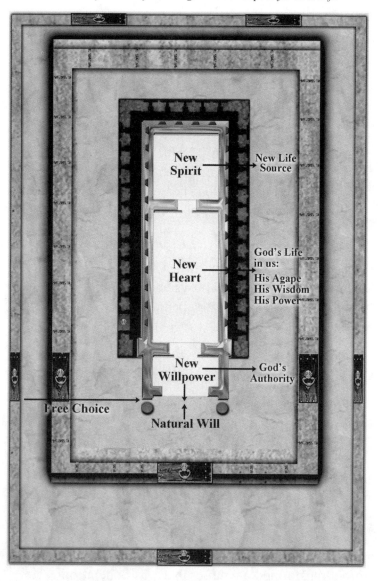

Chart 5

need of transformation. The only life that now exists <u>in</u> our hearts, if we are born again, is God's Life. Our job is simply to learn *how* to let it <u>out</u>.

## New Willpower

### CHART 5: New Spirit, Heart and Willpower

Remember in the last chapter we said that our choice or our willpower is the *key* to our Christian walk and our being able to reflect Him in all we do. The Greek word for willpower is *dianoia*, which means our will and the power to perform it. Again, this is the critical point because what we choose, moment by moment, determines *whose life* will be lived in our souls; either God's from our new heart or our own from our soul. We'll spend the entire next chapter exploring this area of our will.

Our willpower is what enables us to put forth God's Life from our hearts into our lives. If you look at the chart, you'll see that our willpower is like the passageway, the doorway or the gateway for God's Life in our hearts to flow out into our lives. Now, this passageway or doorway can be open so God's Life can freely flow, or it can be closed and thus God's Life quenched and blocked.

The thing that opens or shuts this passageway is our own moment-by-moment choice. God has given us the freedom either to choose to follow what He has shown us and trust in His Power to perform it in our lives; thus, allowing His Spirit to flow. Or the freedom to choose to follow what we think, feel, and desire, and trust in our own ability and power to perform it in our lives; thus, quenching, blocking and greasing over God's Spirit in our heart. In other words, as Christians we have the free choice to follow what God wants–regardless of what we think or feel–and say as Jesus did, "not my will, but thine." (Matthew 26:39) This is known as a **faith choice**. Or we can say, "I'm going to follow what *I* think, what I feel and what *I* want," which is known as a **fleshly choice**.

This is where Pastor Bruce made his fatal error. He began with small, fleshly choices to follow his own desires instead of what he knew God wanted. At first, they weren't really big issues, just small infractions, but after a while these little indiscretions led to bigger ones that ended up completely blocking God's Spirit and preventing God's Life from coming forth at all. The root of Pastor Bruce's fall was simply not being aware of the importance of his moment-by-moment choices.

What happens in situations like this is that Jesus' Life becomes quenched and blocked in our hearts. Psalm 119:70 describes this condition: "Their heart is fat as grease." To me, this describes God's Spirit covered over in our heart with grease and unable to come forth. If this is the case, the glory of God, that Light, is also blocked or prevented from coming forth. So, even though these people are believers and Christ lives within them, His glory cannot come forth.

# Our Soul

See **CHART 6** (Showing the functions of our soul)

Our souls are made up of our natural thoughts, emotions and desires. This is the "self life" that we have so often referred to. (Now, there is also a hidden, subconscious part of our soul—those secret chambers— and we'll talk more about them in just a moment.) But, for the sake of simplicity, think of our souls as the "visible" part of our lives–the *outward expression* of our lives. In other words, our souls are what others see, feel, and hear coming forth from us.

The best analogy I can think of to show the difference between 'heart life' and 'soul life' is with plants in a garden. Our *heart life* is like the root life of those plants. We can't see it—it's underground—but nevertheless, roots are essential to the health and growth of the plants above. Whereas our *soul life* is like the beautiful flowers (or the weeds), that grow above the ground. The flowers (or weeds) are the direct result of the health of the root life. We can visibly see the flowers; we can smell them, feel them, touch them, and enjoy them. Jeremiah says of our soul that it "shall be as a watered garden." (Verse 31:12d)

So, then, our soul is like a neutral area that is either going to be filled with God's Life from our hearts, through

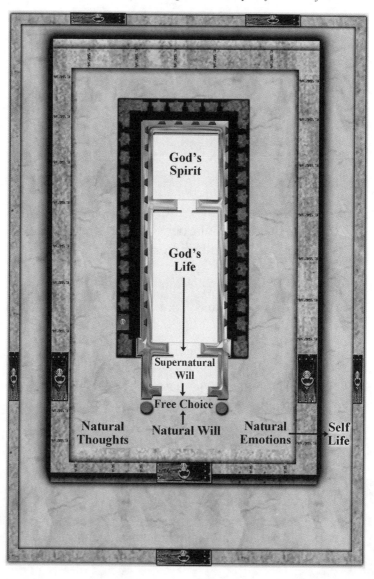

Chart 6

"faith choices"; <u>or</u> filled with self-life–our own thoughts, emotions, and desires, if we have chosen to follow the flesh. The outcome all depends upon what we choose moment by moment.

God's will is that when people look at us, they might see Christ's character, His Likeness and His glory reflected. (John 14:9b)

Let's see what this looks like visually:

### CHART 7: Spirit-filled Soul Glorifying God

Just as Solomon's Temple was filled with God's glory as the Shehinah came forth, so this is the Lord's exact plan for our bodies also. Again, 1 Corinthians 6:20 says: "...your body is the temple of the Holy Ghost which is in you, which ye have of God, and ye are not your own...*therefore glorify God in your body, and in your spirit, which are God's.*"

The Lord wants us filled with His Spirit which can then shine forth in everything we do and everything we say. (Ephesians 5:18) Notice that this temple now looks like a *flashlight*. God's Life is pouring forth from this person's heart through his soul and body. God's supernatural Love in his heart has become his love in his soul; God's wisdom has become his wisdom; and God's power, his own. This is a picture of a "spiritual Christian."

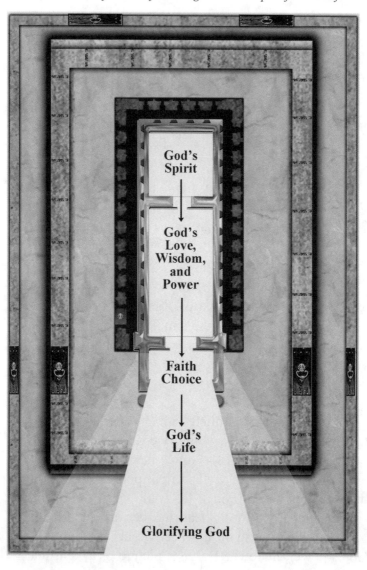

God's
Spirit

God's
Love,
Wisdom,
and
Power

Faith
Choice

God's
Life

Glorifying God

Chart 7          **Spiritual Christian**

And this is also what Luke 11:33 means when it says, "No man, when he hath lighted a candle, putteth it in a secret place, neither under a bushel, but *on a lampstand, that they who come in may see the light.*" This Christian is glorifying God because God's Life is shown forth in all he does.

Remember, the windows of Solomon's temple were designed wider on the inside and narrower on the outside in order to capture the light and radiate it outwards. God wanted His Shekinah Glory–His supernatural light–to be seen for miles around. In like manner, our souls are designed to show forth Jesus' Life from our hearts and radiate it outward. However, if God's Life is quenched because of fleshly or emotional choices, our soul will not show forth His Life, but our own *self-life*, our own thoughts, emotions and desires. If this is the case, this is what we might look like:

## CHART 8: God's Spirit Quenched, Glorifying Self

The soul life coming forth from this Christian is not God's Life as it should be, but his own self-life. He has quenched God's Spirit and His Life at the *choice point.* Consequently, he'll not be able to reflect God's image, as he should. As a result, many will be turned away from the Lord by his phoniness. This is a picture of a "carnal Christian."

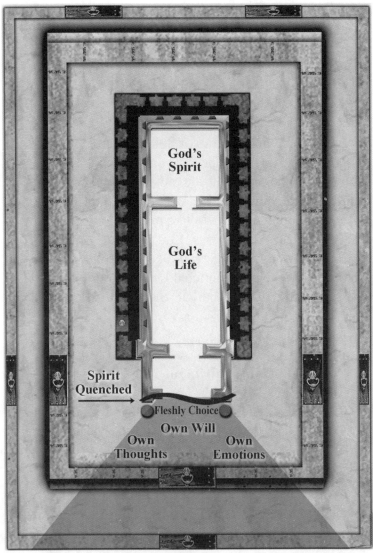

Chart 8                    **Carnal Christian**

I recently spoke with a young man who went to church faithfully for two years, accepted Christ and began to walk in the Spirit. But, when he saw all the hypocrisy around him, he let go. "Where's the real thing?" he asked me. How tragic it is that we continually hear these kinds of reports. Remember this chart. This is what we look like when we make *fleshly* choices to follow our own will rather than God's. We've been "born of the Spirit," yes, but we're certainly not "walking by the Spirit."

This is what Luke 11:33 means when it says, "No man, when he hath lighted a candle, *putteth it in a secret place, neither under a bushel....*" This is God's Life hidden under a bushel. (2 Corinthians 11:18, 30)

## Where Does *Self Life* Come From?

The question then becomes, if we as believers have God's Life in our hearts and this is now our true nature, where does this *self-life* come from? Where does it originate from? It certainly doesn't come from our new heart. Where then? Well, Scripture tells us that when we became born again, we received a new spirit, a new heart and a new willpower, but our soul and body remained the same. It was <u>not</u> changed; it was <u>not</u> renewed; and it was <u>not</u> regenerated.

**CHART 9** (Things in the Hidden Chambers affect our Soul)

Thus, *self-life* comes from the hurts, the resentments, the doubts, the pride, the bitterness, etc. that we have never properly dealt with before, but have instead, stuffed and buried in our secret, hidden chambers which are still a part of our soul. Self-life is triggered when we choose to follow what this buried debris is telling us to do over what God is prompting us to do. Counselors tell us that everything we think, say, and do (good or bad) is stored for future use in these secret, hidden chambers deep within us.

God designed the *sanctification* process to teach us how to recognize our self-life, how to deal with it and then, how to allow *His* new Life from our hearts to come forth. Remember, sanctification is simply the process of restoring the image of Christ in us. Many of us, however, have never learned the cleansing steps and, instead, we have just pushed down and buried much of our pain. Thus, we have given the enemy many entrances and footholds in our soul.

This highlights something very important and something we will expand upon later. Any demonic activity that perhaps we were involved in *before* we became believers needs to be exposed, renounced and given over to God so that no strongholds will remain in these hidden chambers to harass us in the future.

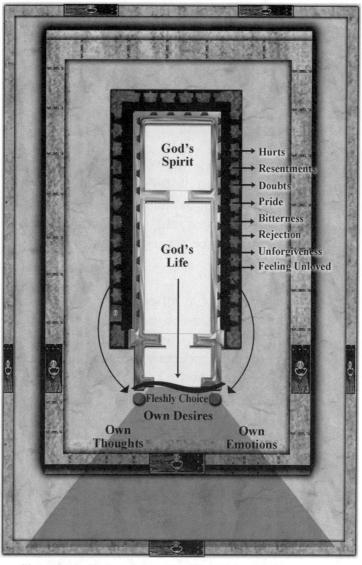

Chart 9    **Reflecting and Glorifying Self**

Thousands of Christians live under such bondage from these kinds of past chains and, thus, never seem to reach the freedom in Christ that they so desire.

We'll speak more about "strongholds" in Chapter 7.

## Our Bodies

Finally, our bodies are the "vehicles" (or the carriers) for the expression of God's Life and His glory. In other words, we need a soul in order to express life and we need a body to carry that soul. Thus, our souls and our bodies really cannot be separated. Together they are called "the flesh."

We can be Christians all our lives yet because we continue to make *fleshly choices* no one will ever see Christ's Life in us. His Life will be quenched and no one will ever see the difference between us and our neighbors who may not even know the Lord.

This is exactly what a "hypocrite" is–a Christian who says all the right things but whose actions don't match his words. He *says* he is a Christian, and yet his life shows something totally different. He knows that Jesus is the answer, but his life doesn't prove it. This is the reason why the Christian body is having such a difficult time these days. Many of us have become hypocrites–living two lives. Jesus' Life is in our hearts, but self-life is what is shown from our souls. Again, a carnal Christian.

# God's Will

Consequently, just as Solomon's Temple in 1 Kings 8: 10-11 and 2 Chronicles 5:13-14 was filled from the *inside out* with God's Glory as He came forth from the Holy of Holies, so this is God's exact purpose for us. Daily we are to allow God's Spirit to issue forth from the Holy of Holies of our hearts, fill our souls and glorify God in our bodies. (Remember **CHART 7,** page 104).

This is what John 7:38 is referring to when it says, "He that believeth on Me, as the Scripture hath said, *out of his belly shall flow rivers of living water.*"

Unfortunately, this out flowing is not a one-time event. It's a moment-by-moment choice to be filled with His Spirit and to let it flow outward. Ephesians 5:17-18 expresses it this way: "Be ye not unwise, but understanding what the will of the Lord is...be filled with the Spirit [all day long, every day]."

# Single-mindedness vs. Double-mindedness

The Bible refers to this infilling and out flowing event as being *"single-minded"* or "one-souled." Meaning that only *one life* is being lived here. Because we are cleansed, God's Life is freely coming forth from our hearts, filling our souls and producing godly life actions. At this moment, we are "living the truth" because our words and deeds match. There's not any hypocrisy. We're not only "born of the Spirit," we're also "walking by the Spirit."

However, when we *don't* choose to *put off* the sin and self in our lives, God's Spirit will be quenched and self-life will show forth. At this point, we will be "*double-minded*" or "twice-souled." Meaning two lives are being lived here. See CHART 8 again. God's Life is still in our hearts, but it's quenched. Thus, self-life has taken over in our souls. Because we have chosen to follow our own lusts, hurts, frustration, anger, guilt and etc., over what God has told us, God's Life is blocked and self-centered life actions are produced.

*The bottom line is that we can be Christians all of our lives, with God's Life in our hearts, and yet because we continue to make fleshly and emotional choices to follow what we think, feel and desire over what God is prompting us to do, God's Life in us will be quenched. Thus, no one will ever see the difference between us and non-believers.*

Titus 1:16 confirms this, "They profess that they know God, but in works they deny Him." We also see this in Luke 11:17: "Every kingdom divided against itself is brought to desolation; and a house divided against a house falleth."

*Double-mindedness, therefore, is the enemy's game plan*. He will do everything he can to get us to act upon what we are feeling, what we are thinking and what others are telling us, rather than letting us make "faith choices" to cleanse ourselves so that God's Life can come forth. The enemy knows that double-mindedness not only immediately quenches God's Life in us, but it also prevents the Gospel from being passed on.

Consequently, Satan revels in our double-mindedness! He knows that double-mindedness keeps us bound by our hurts and wounds, gives him an "open door" and destroys our witness.

## Be a Light

Luke 11:33-36, that we talked about just a moment ago, describes both single-mindedness and double-mindedness. Let's read the entire passage: "No man, when he hath lighted a candle, putteth it in a secret place, neither under a bushel, but on a candlestick, that they which come in may see the light. The light of the body is the eye: therefore when thine eye is single [*single-minded*], thy whole body also is full of light; but when thine eye is evil [*double-minded*], thy body also is full of darkness. Take heed therefore, that the light which is in thee be not darkness [covered over]. If thy whole body therefore be full of light, having no part dark, the whole shall be full of light, as when the bright shining of a candle doth give thee light."

Jesus' Life is the Light that Luke is talking about here.[16]  Our goal and purpose as Christians is not only be to be filled with that Light, but also to let that Light shine forth to others.  As Psalm 80:1d says, "Thou that dwellest between the cherubims, *shine forth*."

We're not to *hide that light under a bushel* (self-life), but *put it on a lampstand where <u>all</u> can see it.*

Turn back to **CHART 7**  (page 104)

This passage in Luke says that when we are "single-minded," we will have a *body full of light* (i.e., Jesus' Life will exude from us like a flashlight).  His Life will be on a lampstand where all can see it.  This is a picture of a spiritual Christian putting off all his own sin and self, putting on Christ, and then glorifying Him in all he does.

However, turn back to **CHART 8**  (page 106)

This is a double-minded, carnal Christian who has a *body full of darkness.*  Such Christians are <u>not</u> dealing with their own sin and self, nor are they reflecting or glorifying the Lord.  They have chosen instead to hold on to their hurts, resentments, bitterness, anger, etc., and these things have quenched God's Spirit in them.  At this point, not only is all personal communication and leading from the Lord choked out and blocked, but it also causes them to become insensitive and unfeeling towards others.  This is what forces them to *live a lie.*  Saying they are

Christians, but their actions loudly disproving it. This is why so many of us end up wearing "masks" and facades. We can't let others see that it's not really working for us and we really don't understand why.

As Isaiah 59:10 describes this state of mind, "We grope for the wall like the blind, and we grope as if we had no *eyes*."

This is also why many Christians get "tired" of *playing* at being Christian. They have worked hard at living Christ's Life for Him–copying Him and imitating Him–rather than simply exchanging lives with Him so that *He can live His Life out through them*.

Hopefully, this little visual overview will help you understand the continual war that goes on *in us* between our flesh and the Spirit of God and help you to see why we are often unable to glorify the Lord. The more we can visualize what actually occurs when we quench God's Spirit in us (**CHART 8**), the more we'll realize the importance of making moment-by-moment faith choices. Then, as Luke says, "will our loins be girded about [with truth] and *our lights burning*." (12:35) Remember **CHART 7**.

# Chapter Three Questions

1) What makes Solomon's Temple so unique and so different from all the other temples of worship? (1 Chronicles 28:11-12, 19; Exodus 25:22)


2) Solomon's Temple was built for what purpose?


3) God's Spirit now dwells where?  What's His purpose? (1 Corinthians 3:16; 6:19-29; 2 Corinthians 6:16)


4) When we became born again, what areas of our body are automatically changed? (Ezekiel 36:26-27)


5) Define our spirit, heart and willpower.


6) What then is our soul?


7) We spoke of "self-life". Where does it come from?

8) What is God's will for us as the temple of the
   Holy Spirit? (1 Kings 8:10-11;
   2 Chronicles 5:13-14; John 7:38)


9) Contrast "single-mindedness" with "double-
   mindedness." (Luke 11:34,17; Titus 1:16)


10) Explain why so many Christians get tired of
    "playing at being a Christian," of copying
    Christ and of imitating Him?

# Warfare Prayer

Dearest Lord: I desire to be a reflection of Your image so that my family, friends and others will see You in me and want what I have. Therefore, I choose to give You anything in me that would prevent my hearing directly from Your Spirit. I present my body as a living sacrifice, holy, acceptable unto You, which is my reasonable service. And I choose *not* to be conformed to this world but to be transformed (into Your image) by the renewing of my mind that I may prove what is Your good, acceptable and perfect will. (Romans 12:1-2)

I choose to "put on" the whole armor of God that I might be able to stand against the wiles of the enemy, having done all to stand strong. First of all, I choose to stand by having my loins girt about with truth and having on the breastplate of righteousness and Love guarding my heart. Next, I choose to shod my feet with the preparation of the Gospel of peace. *Above all, I take up the shield of faith by which I can quench all the fiery darts of the enemy.* (Ephesians 6:13-17)

# Chapter Four
## How to Choose to Follow the Spirit

## Our Choice

This will be the most important chapter in this book. Because learning how to make faith choices to follow the Spirit's leading regardless of how we feel or think is the *key* to our entire Christian walk. Faith, itself, is simply a series of on-going choices.

Scripture tells us that when we are "born again" we not only receive a *new* spirit and a *new* heart, but we also receive a *new* supernatural willpower–a supernatural empowering of the Holy Spirit called in the Greek, *dianoia.* As we saw last chapter, this is the authority and power that God gives us in order to do things we don't naturally *feel*, don't want to do and don't think will work. This is His God-given power to set ourselves aside and choose His will regardless of our own thoughts and emotions. This kind of a choice enables us to totally give ourselves over to Him and do what He is calling us to do–even if it's the last thing in the world we "feel" like doing. This is the heart of Biblical Christianity.

As previously mentioned, we have a constant choice as to whom we will yield our members. Romans 6:12-13 says, "Let not sin therefore reign in your mortal body, that ye should obey it in the lusts thereof. Neither yield ye your members as instruments of unrighteousness unto sin: but yield yourselves unto God, as those that are alive from the dead, and your members as instruments of righteousness unto God." This Scripture tells us we will either yield them to God to accomplish His will through us, or we will yield ourselves to do our own pleasure. It's our willpower—our moment-by-moment choice—that will determine this, and ultimately determine *whose life* will be shown forth in our souls. If we choose to yield ourselves to God, His Life will be seen. (**CHART 7**) If we choose to yield ourselves to the flesh, self-life will be seen. (**CHART 8**)

God has all the Love, wisdom and power we need. However, the choice to be a cleansed vessel through which He can work these things is always ours.

## Contrary Choices

Our willpower has two parts to it: 1) We have *God's supernatural will and power*, which gives us His counsel as to what His will is and His power to perform that will in our lives; and 2) We also have the *free choice* to either follow what God has shown us and depend upon His ability to perform it in our lives or we can choose to follow our own desires and trust in our own ability to perform it in our lives.

Supernatural willpower means the authority and power of God to enable us to make a *contrary choice–a choice that goes against what we naturally think, feel, and desire.* That's why I call it a "contrary choice." It's a faith choice or a non-feeling choice. In other words, it's a choice to walk by faith, not by sight. 2 Corinthians 8:11 validates this: "As there was a readiness to will, so there may be a performance also."

It's interesting because we are so programmed from youth to "feel" everything we choose. And when we don't feel our choices, we don't think they're genuine. However, in God's Kingdom this is <u>not</u> the case. Born-again believers possess the authority and power of God to *go against* what we naturally think and feel. God, then, will take it from there. *Therefore, Christians are the only ones who possess a supernatural power within them to perform something different from what they naturally think, feel, and desire.*

Now, certainly, non-believers have a choice to decide what they want to do. But *none of them have the authority to choose to go against how they feel, what they think, and what they desire, because they don't possess another power within them to perform anything different.* Christians, on the other hand, do! And this is what makes us so different from non-believers, who don't really have any other choice but to follow what their flesh is telling them (i.e., they must "go with the flow"). Even though they might desperately want to change and go a different direction, they are unable to. They don't possess the authority or the ability within themselves to do so. Thus, in reality, they don't have any other choice but to follow what their own thoughts, emotions and desires are telling them.

Christians, however, do! Because of the Spirit of God in us, we have <u>His</u> authority to say "not my will but Thine," and then His power to give our negative thoughts and emotions over to Him. Thankfully—we don't have to be carried on by the tide of emotion like non-believers. We have Christ's authority to choose His will and His power to perform that will in our lives.

Philippians 2:13 tells us that "it is God who worketh in you both *to will* and *to do* of His good pleasure." And also in 1 Corinthians 7:37, it assures us that we have power over our own wills.

## Example of a Difficult Faith Choice

Here's a personal example.

Seven years ago, our precious son Chip, only 39 years old, went home to be with the Lord. He had simply gone out for a jog one Saturday afternoon and ended up dying from a massive heart attack. He left behind a beautiful young wife and two babies. Of course, the devastation for all of us was beyond description. Chip was the hub around which all of our family lived.

Just 20 days after Chip passed on, there was a retreat scheduled in Chicago where I was to speak. I couldn't get out of it because it would have been too short of a notice to cancel. On the airplane going to Chicago, I told God I had absolutely *nothing* at all to give these women. I was grieving and totally empty, <u>but</u> I knew <u>He</u> must have a purpose for all of this and I was willing to simply be an open vessel.

On the plane I opened up the file for the seminar and immediately noticed a letter from a woman named Shar, whom I had corresponded with a couple of times. Three years previously, Shar had lost her oldest son in a horrible automobile accident. He was only 20 at the time but loved the Lord with all his heart. Shar had been a Christian for years, had taught numerous Bible studies, and had exhorted many others to know Christ. But, losing her son had absolutely crushed her. She could not understand how a loving God would allow such a tragedy to happen to a family who loved Him so much.

The more she questioned God, the more doubt and unbelief grew in her soul. Eventually, Shar found herself at the lowest point in her walk with the Lord, totally defeated and despairing. When she prayed she couldn't hear His voice. When she read the Bible, the enemy twisted its meaning to convey something totally opposite from what was intended. And, when she attended Bible Studies, she didn't get anything out of them. So she just stopped praying, stopped reading and stopped going. She totally gave up! She felt God had covered Himself with a cloud and had abandoned her in her deepest need.

Shar became so depressed that she wanted to die. She no longer cared about anything or anyone. She dropped out of church, stopped seeing her friends and quit all social activities.

The coming seminar "happened" to be at her home church.

Suddenly, I knew *why* God was sending me there.

The Lord, in His Love, had arranged this particular weekend not only to minister to me, but also to minister to Shar. He wanted to show her just how much He loved her, and to what extreme He would go to communicate that Love to her.

I had last corresponded with Shar about a year *before* Chip died. In my letters I encouraged her as much as I possibly could and included passages like Romans 8: 28: "all things work together for good to those who love God." However at that time, I really could not identify with her because I had never walked in her shoes. *One year later, however, things radically changed–Chip died.*

When I arrived in Chicago, I immediately called Shar and asked if she was going to the meeting that night. She said "no" and explained why. Then I told her about Chip. She had not heard. She began to cry. I too, sobbed. But I told her that God had arranged this weekend for both of us and that He had sent me especially to her. He wanted the two of us, that very night, to go out under the stars and relinquish our sons over to Him, laying them at the Cross.

Shar came. And, after the seminar was over, the two of us went outside, sat under the stars and out of obedience (because neither of us felt like it) gave our sons back to the Creator. The love that flowed between us and the Love we experienced from the Lord at that moment is something I will never forget. It was Christ's Love, His life, flowing between us, ministering to us, encouraging us and lifting us up. We felt Jesus Himself, had come and touched us.

Shar is now back in church and fellowshipping and, the last I heard, doing very well. God allowed still another very difficult night season in her life but from what I hear, she has received it from God's hands and is glorifying Him through it.

Faith choices allow us to embrace whatever trials God sends our way and yet, still be able to display His Love in midst of them.

# Not My Will, but Thine

True Christianity is such an incredibly freeing walk, in that we can be honest with God and confess things like: "I'm afraid. I can't do this. I don't love this person anymore. I don't want to forgive him. I don't feel Your Presence. I am doubtful that You are leading me to do this. I don't understand what You are doing. I am fearful of what is going to happen, etc." But, by faith, we can give these negative thoughts over to the Lord and know that we have <u>His</u> authority to say, "not my will, but Thine," and then <u>His</u> power to perform that will in our life. (Matthew 26:39) Then, we can be assured that in God's perfect timing, He will *align* our feelings to match the faith choices we have made.

What's so incredible about making these kinds of *contrary choices* is that God does, in His timing and in His Way, not only change our negative thoughts and emotions to match what we have chosen, but He also restores our joy. In other words, if we are just willing to make the right choices, He will give us the Love, wisdom and power we need to go on with our lives.

Professional counselors will tell us that no matter how hard we try, it's impossible to change our own feelings. Therefore, the only way we can implement a change in how we feel is to release our emotions to God by means of a faith choice.

Our new supernatural willpower is simply God's authority and power to choose His will over our own thoughts, emotions, and desires (our self-life). And, to me, *this is the most incredible gift of all. I don't have to "feel" my choices; I just have to be willing to make them. God then does the rest.*

## An Example: Anna

Here's another remarkable real-life example. This is a letter from a friend of mine who had just received some horrific news and how she handled it. As you read her letter, think about how you might have handled the situation.

"It was the last day of our trip home to Florida to visit our family and I was at my husband's parents' house where we'd always stayed, packing alone. All the kids were at the beach and Ken, my husband, was out fishing with two brothers-in-law.

"The Lord had me stay home alone and soon I would find out why. As I was packing, the Holy Spirit led me to Ken's suitcase and had me lift up the bottom of the inside of it to find an address book with over two pages of women's names and their descriptions. At first, I froze, as tears of unbelief welled up deep inside of me. *I wanted to run* (I felt like I had finally found my ticket out of a very unhappy marriage), but the still, small voice of the Spirit of God within constrained me. *'Remember, I'm in control,'* He said. *'How you handle this and the choices you make are critical. Choose to walk by faith, not your feelings, and your life will change.'*

"I called a friend and placed myself under her accountability and received some wise counsel as to how to proceed. My husband arrived home shortly after that and with the book in hand, I asked him if this was happening now. He said, 'yes.' He just looked at me and said, 'I am going to hell. You know Jesus, will you please pray for me!'

"Those were perhaps the most honest words I have ever heard him say. So, I did pray and I asked God, 'May *Your* will and not *mine* be done. I give this to You and it is now in Your hands.' (My own feelings inside were screaming, 'run, get out, this is your chance!' But I chose, by faith, to really mean what I had said in my prayer.)

"Immediately, Ken began to confess everything. He took the book from my hands, ran into the adjoining bathroom and lit it on fire. When he came back he said, 'It is time to expose my sin.'

"A dear pastor that we know came over that night and spent three hours with Ken out in the street. Later, the pastor asked me to come out and told me that, 'Ken has just had a Damascus Road experience.' I wouldn't have believed him, except that I had prayed those very same words for my husband many times. And in a prayer meeting just a month earlier, someone gave me a word for my husband, using 'the Damascus Road' analogy. Then the pastor said to me, 'God has heard your prayer. Ken was saved tonight and baptized out in that street.' Well, you can imagine how I was feeling!

"The next few weeks involved a lot of pain, but an unfolding of the glory of God like I have never seen before. Ken confessed to all the men he is close to. He confessed to our four teenage children, my mom, sisters and two pastor friends that he was a false convert living a life headed for hell. He even named all his sins sparing the grossness of the details to protect their imaginations. Telling the children was the hardest of all. They each began to cry. They thought their dad *was* a Christian. But God's glory shined, even through this, and He began to heal all of our hearts.

"Eventually, Ken asked me to marry him again and our lives have never been the same. He now calls me from his car and holds the phone up to the marriage tapes he is listening to, so I can hear. For the first time in 19 years, we are experiencing the oneness in the Spirit that God so desires. We are continually in the Word and praying together. We have had more conversation in the past year than we've had in all our 19 years put together. Our children are alive as never before. I didn't realize till now that they, too, were dying.

"There is so much more to share, but God has given me a heart filled with the joy that is born out of pain, a great new love for my Savior and a hunger to know God's Love in an even deeper way. Isn't He wonderful!"

What makes the above story so miraculous is that, in spite of how Anna felt, in spite of what she thought and in spite of what she wanted, she chose to trust God and, by faith, do His will. God then supernaturally changed her feelings to align with her choices and restored her marriage. This story is miraculous because Anna made non-feeling choices that allowed God to intervene and thus, change the course of her life.

## What Would You Have Done?

What would have happened had Anna chosen not to follow God but to follow her own justified feelings? She would have immediately split with Ken and her story would have had a very different ending. Our choices are critical, because if we can make choices by faith, they can *change the course of our lives*!

Life is simply a series of ongoing choices. For the non-believer, it's a daily choice of what he wants to do, how he feels and what he thinks. However, for the believer, it's a totally different scenario! It's a moment-by-moment choice to either follow his own fleshly desires (just like a non-believer), or to say like Jesus, "not My will but Thine" and follow what God desires.

Faith is being fully persuaded that God is able to do all that He has promised. Faith is radical reliance upon God and it comes in the form of a choice. In fact, we must often choose 100 times a day to be fully persuaded the Lord will do as He says. Therefore, *real faith is a series of moment-by-moment choices to believe God even when everything in our lives is screaming just the opposite.*

Again, 2 Corinthians 4:10-11, "Always bearing about in the body the dying of the Lord Jesus, that the life also of Jesus might be made manifest in our body. For we which live are always delivered unto death for Jesus' sake [death of self-life so] that the life also of Jesus might be made manifest in our mortal flesh."

## The Key to Life

Our choice, then, is the key to our life. Our choice is what enables us to put God's Life from our hearts out into our souls. It's the passageway, the doorway or the gateway. This passageway can be *opened*, so God's Life can flow easily (Remember **CHART 7**); <u>or</u> it can be *closed*, so God's Life will be quenched and blocked. (Remember **CHART 8**).

Remember the Greek word for our willpower? It's *dianoia*. And, it's interesting because, *dia* means "channel" and *noya* means "of the mind." And this is exactly what our willpower is–the channel, or the conduit, for God's Spirit to flow from our hearts out into our lives.

Consequently, our willpower or our choice, is the determining factor as to whose life will be lived in our soul. Faith choices allow God's Life to come forth; whereas emotional choices quench God's Life. So, it all boils down to this: Are you willing to set aside what you think, feel and want in order to do what God asks? Or will you yield yourself to your own thoughts and emotions and do what *you* want?

Remember Anna's dilemma? She wanted to run from her husband and the situation because it was so painful. And we could all identify with her feelings. But, God's Spirit ministered to her that <u>He</u> was still in control and that He wanted her to remain in the marriage and see it through. He exhorted her that if she chose to walk by faith, her life would change. And it did!

Our Christian life is <u>not</u> determined by our circumstances, our church attendance, our social standing, our finances or even our belief systems, but the character of our life is determined by the daily choices we make. In other words, our new willpower gives us the authority and power of God to *"go against the tide"*—to set ourselves aside and follow the Lord, regardless of how we feel, what we want or what we think. *Our choice is the critical crossroads of our lives.*

Sin isn't birthed in our mind or in our body; it's begun within our will! Therefore, God has given us a fearful and awesome responsibility, because what we choose determines the degree of our sanctification. *Faith choices* allow God's Life, from our hearts, to flow out into our lives; whereas, *fleshly choices* quench God's Life and block it from coming forth.

## *Exousia*

The Greek word for this "free choice" decision is *exousia*, which means, "it is permitted." *Exousia* implies that we have the authority and the word of the person in charge (which is God) to choose something we don't feel; and we also have <u>His</u> power and ability to implement that choice in our lives. What this says is that, as Christians, we have the constant choice either to "relinquish ourselves" and do what God wants <u>or</u> "hold on to ourselves" and do what we please.

Jesus talks about *exousia* in John 10:17-18: "Therefore doth My Father love Me, because I lay down My life, that I might take it again. No man taketh it from Me, but I lay it down of Myself. I have power to lay it down, and I have power to take it again."

In Matthew 16:19, Jesus promises us, "I will give unto thee the keys of the kingdom of heaven: and whatsoever thou shalt bind on earth shall be bound in heaven: and whatsoever thou shalt loose on earth shall be loosed in heaven."

Often we associate this Scripture with binding and loosing the enemy. But, in a personal sense, to bind literally means to "prohibit or forbid self" and to loose means to "permit or to allow self." This Scripture is saying that we, as Christians, possess the authority and the power of God to either "forbid self" (set self aside) and walk after the Spirit, or to "allow self" (let self reign) and walk after the flesh. We'll talk more about this in Chapter Seven.

## Maturity in Christ

The mature Christian is one who recognizes his self-life and makes the appropriate choices to give it over to God. Maturity in Christ is not knowing an abundance of theological facts, going to church regularly, teaching Bible studies or even writing books. Maturity in Christ is simply making the right faith choice to cleanse ourselves of all God shows us, so that His Life can come forth. In other words, the people who are mature are the ones who are constantly watching for and recognizing their own sin. *They are mature because they know how to recognize the flesh and how to make choices to hand it over to God.*

One of the ways we can tell how mature in the Lord we are is by how sensitive we are to seeing our own sin. And, I find this to be so true. The longer I am with the Lord, the more sin and self I see in me.

Naturally, even as Christians, we are still full of *self*–our own natural thoughts, emotions and desires—especially in trials. Some of these thoughts and emotions *are* fully "justified" by the world's standards. But by God's standards, *because we hold on to them, mull them over in our minds and then act upon them, these negative thoughts and emotions end up quenching God's Spirit in us.* If we can learn to give our real feelings and thoughts over to God, like Anna in the previous story, and choose by faith to follow God's will, then He will align our feelings with our faith choices and make us genuine.

This is what maturity in Christ is all about.

## Learning to Deny Self

A Scripture that goes along with giving our thoughts and feelings to God is Matthew 16:24: "If any man will come after Me, *let him deny himself, take up his cross, and follow* Me." (Mark 8:34; Luke 9:23)

To *deny* in the above Scripture does not mean to push down and bury real feelings and negate their existence. Many of us have been doing this out of habit because we've been taught that we're <u>not</u> supposed to feel these negative things. However, one of the benefits of being in Christ is that we have the freedom to be honest. We can acknowledge our real thoughts and emotions even if they are bad, confess and repent of them, give them over to the Lord, and, then, be free of them altogether.

Thus, "to deny" in this context means to *bar ourselves or prevent ourselves from following what we naturally think and feel.* We're all human and we will all have negative thoughts and feelings until the day we see Jesus. Denying ourselves simply means choosing not to follow these things.

Thus, it's important that when we look at our real thoughts and feelings that we call them for what they are, so that we will know exactly what to give over to the Lord. We must learn to *bar ourselves* or *prevent ourselves* from following what these negative elements of our lives are telling us and, instead, learn to give them to the Lord. Then we will be free to follow what He wants. (We will discuss the exact steps of doing this next chapter.)

*Self-denial, therefore, is the law of the Christian life.* We are to deny our self, pick up our cross and follow Him. The Cross is the chief mark of a Christian. We are not to glory in anything, except in the Cross of Christ. (Galatians 6:14) Even though our old man has been positionally crucified, as we said before he is still not dead. Daily, the old nature must be nailed to the cross, which means dying to our self-life.

## Suffering For Christ

It's difficult to talk about denying self and the Cross without at least mentioning the principle of suffering for Christ. It's interesting, because throughout Scripture "glorifying the Lord" and "suffering for Him" always seem to be linked. It's a pattern that we see over and over again. (See John 11:1-4) *Indeed, glorifying the Lord seems to be the result of suffering for Him.* (1 Peter 1:11)

Suffering simple means choosing to bar ourselves from following what we think, feel and want and, instead, choosing to do what God wants. In other words, suffering often occurs as a result of denying ourselves. Just as Jesus valiantly chose to set Himself aside, and endure the Cross and the suffering that followed *because it was the Father's will.* (Matthew 26:39; Philippians 2:5-8) So we, too, often suffer when we choose to deny ourselves, pick up our cross and follow Him. Anna is a good example. The *flesh* shrinks from this kind of suffering, but the spirit knows that often it's the *only* way to life. Scripture tells us that we are made perfect through suffering. James 1: 2-4 confirms this: "My brethren, count it all joy, when you fall into various trials, knowing this, that the trying of your faith worketh patience. But let patience have her perfect work, *that you may be perfect and entire, lacking nothing.*"

2 Timothy 2:12 goes even farther by saying that if we <u>don't</u> suffer for Christ–if we don't deny ourselves–then we won't reign with Him. "*If* we suffer, we shall also reign with Him; if we deny Him, He will also deny us."

# The Purpose of Suffering

Those of us who have lived long enough understand that *life itself includes suffering.* The 9th chapter of Ecclesiastes 9 points us to the truth that "all things come alike to all." Misfortune and evil and calamity and "time and chance" happen to everyone. (verses 2, 11) However, we also know that God is above all these things and He will use any or all of them as He sees fit to accomplish His perfect will in our lives.

Suffering can be a result of our own sin, the sins of others, the schemes of Satan or from the fallen state of the human race. Here are a few other reasons suffering occurs:

1) To produce brokenness.
2) To destroy anything in our lives that is worthless, empty and steering us in the wrong direction.
3) To make us more pliable.
4) To make us more Christ-like.
5) To endow us with more power.
6) To experience the "fellowship of His sufferings," and
7) To teach us how to help others, by our own experiences.

Another of God's purposes for suffering is to highlight the things in our own lives that must be dealt with. He wants us to make an honest self-evaluation of ourselves, which in turn, should lead us to confession, repentance and a change of lifestyle.

"And thou shalt remember all the way which the Lord thy God led thee these forty years in the wilderness, *to humble thee, and to test thee, to know what was in thine heart*, whether thou wouldest keep His commandments, or not." (Deuteronomy 8:2)

God put the book of Job, the longest book of the Bible, right in the center of the Bible for a very good reason: it's an example of *faith in the night seasons and the determination never to give up.* God intends for all of us to use this book as a "road map" through the dark times, always keeping in mind that at the end of the road, *Job finally "saw" himself and God as he never had before, changing his life forever.* (Job 42:5)

## Conformed to His Death

I'd like to expand on one of the before mentioned purposes for suffering. We said that one of the reasons God allows suffering in our lives is so that we might experience the "fellowship of His sufferings." Let's read exactly what the Bible says about this: "...That I may know Him, and the power of His resurrection, *and the fellowship of His sufferings, [and by this] being made conformable unto His death.*" (Philippians 3:10)

Note that this Scripture not only talks about the power of His resurrection and the fellowship of the Lord's suffering, but it also mentions that we are to be made "*conformable unto His death.*" Now, I certainly want to know Him and experience the power of His resurrection, but what I never realized before was that the only way that would ever happen is *after* I am conformed to His death. In other words, **spiritual death must precede spiritual life!**

The Living Bible translates "being conformed to His death" as *finding out what it means to suffer and die with Him.* It means personally walking out Christ's death in our own lives. It means, "dying daily," as Paul says in 1 Corinthians 15:31. It means constantly setting aside our own thoughts, emotions and desires and all our own self-centered ways (belief systems, expectations, etc.) that are contrary to His, so that His Life from our heart can come forth. It's called "dying to self."

Philippians 3:10 is saying that the only way to truly "know" Him and the power of His resurrection is by *first* experiencing the fellowship of His sufferings in our life and *by being conformed unto His death.* Again, spiritual death must precede spiritual life. We must *decrease*, so that He can increase. (John 3:30) We must be stripped of self, so that we can then be filled with Him.

## The Fellowship of the Unashamed

Someone just sent me a beautiful piece of prose called *The Fellowship of the Unashamed* by a young Zimbabwe pastor who was martyred for his faith in Christ. Listen:

"The dye has been cast. The decision has been made. I have stepped over the line. I won't look back, let up, slow down or back away. My past is redeemed, my present makes sense, my future is secure. I am finished and done with low living, sight walking, small planning, smooth knees, colorless dreams, tame visions, mundane talking, cheap giving and dwarfed goals.

"I no longer need preeminence, prosperity, position, promotions, plaudits or popularity. I don't have to be right, first, tops, recognized, praised, regarded or rewarded. I now live by faith, lean on His presence, walk with patience, live by prayer and labor with power. My face is set. My gait is fast. My goal is heaven. My road is narrow. My way is rough. My companions are few. My Guide is reliable. My mission is clear. I cannot be bought, compromised, detoured, lured away, turned back, deluded or delayed. I will not flinch in the face of sacrifice, hesitate in the presence of adversity, negotiate at the table of the enemy, ponder at the pool of popularity, or meander in the maze of mediocrity. I won't give up, shut up, let up, until I have stayed up, prayed up, stored up, paid up and spoken up for the cause of Christ.

"I am a disciple of Jesus Christ. I must go till He comes, give till I drop, preach till all know and work till He stops me, and when He comes for His own, He will have no problem recognizing me. My banner is clear. I am part of the fellowship of the unashamed."

May we all passionately say these same words and mean them with the same conviction as this dear pastor.

## God's Will

God's will for <u>all</u> believers is that we should be "conformed into the image of His Son" as Romans 8: 29 tells us. This is God's basic will and the goal of our instruction. In other words, He wants to reproduce His Life and His Love in us. Many of us talk very openly about this and pray for it in our own lives. However, what we don't realize is that *in order to be conformed into His image, we must <u>first</u> be conformed to His death*. This is exactly what Philippians is telling us.

Ultimately, in order to experience the fullness of Christ, we must each personally experience our own Garden of Gethesmane and our own Calvary. (Philippians 1:29) Throughout Scripture, nothing is made alive or quickened unless it first dies. Philippians 2:5-9 gives us Christ's example:

"Let this mind be in you, which was also in Christ Jesus: Who, being in the form of God, thought it not robbery to be equal with God: But made Himself of no reputation, and took upon Him the form of a servant, and was made in the likeness of men: And being found in fashion as a man, He humbled Himself, and became *obedient unto death*, even the death of the cross. Wherefore God also hath highly exalted Him, and given Him a Name which is above every name."

Romans 6:5 also highlights this same teaching: "For if we have been planted together in the likeness of His death, we shall be also in the likeness of His resurrection."

How easy it is for us to simply *preach,* "Christ crucified." The question we must always come back to is, how can we preach Christ crucified if we don't really live it? There's no way we can communicate it, if we have not personally lived it out in our lives first! Our daily prayer should be what Paul prayed in Corinthians, that we would know nothing but Christ crucified and that death would work in us, so that His life could be formed in others. (2 Corinthians 4:12)

Just as Calvary preceded Pentecost, so death with Christ always precedes the fullness of the Spirit. Jesus' cross must become our cross, so that what others see and hear in us will truly bear the marks of Jesus' character.

As Paul declares in Galatians 6:17, "I bear in my body the marks of the Lord Jesus." We should be able to say the same. Only through suffering can we be perfected, completed and made whole. God's glory is only shared by those who are willing to suffer with Him. (1 Peter 4: 14; Romans 8:18)

## Carved into His Image

The other night, I was home reading Isaiah 64:4, "For since the beginning of the world men have not heard, nor perceived by the ear, neither hath the eye seen, O God, beside Thee, what He hath prepared for him that *waiteth* for Him." And the word *waiteth* just popped off the page.

This Scripture tells us that all these wonderful things will happen to the believer who "waits" for the Lord. What does that really mean?

Well, you know me and treasure hunts! I love them.

I found this same Scripture in the New Testament in 1 Corinthians 2:9. Only here the phrase is not "those that wait for Him," but "those that love Him"–those who totally give themselves over to Him. This even peaked my interest all the more. What does it mean to wait for Him?

I was fascinated to discover that the word "wait" (*chakah*) in the Hebrew means, "to adhere to," "to pierce," or "carve or etch an image into." Wow! Then it hit me. *God has prepared something beyond imagining to those who have been carved, sculpted and etched into His image.* The soulish things in their life have been cut away and only Jesus' image is left.

In the same chapter of Isaiah where we find the Scripture "those that wait upon the Lord," we also find the Scripture that talks about the Lord being the potter and we the clay, confirming that He molds, shapes and patiently carves us into His image. (Isaiah 64:8)

## Process of Sanctification

God has chosen us to "salvation through sanctification of the Spirit." (2 Thessalonians 2:13) Sanctification again is the process of restoring the image of Christ in us. It's the delicate process of learning how to follow the Spirit's leading, how to be cleansed by the Spirit, how to worship in the Spirit, how to abide in the Spirit, and, finally, how to walk by the Spirit. It's the process of learning how to becoming holy, purified, consecrated and separated unto God. It's simply the means by which our spirit is freed to control every aspect of our lives and the process of learning how to make faith choices, which allow Christ's supernatural Life to come forth.

The word *sanctify* actually comes from the Greek root word *hagion* which means "holy place." This is particularly fascinating because the verb *hagiazo* (to sanctify) is used to describe the gold that adorns the Holy Place of the temple. And it's true, only those who have been sanctified may enter the Holy Place. Sanctification, then, is the removal of anything in our lives that is unrighteous or unholy. (1 Thessalonians 4:3) The root of holiness or sanctification, which interestingly are the same Greek word in Scripture, is co-crucifixion and co-resurrection. (1 Thessalonians 4:3, 7; 5:23) It's the process of destroying the "old man" and replacing it with the image of Christ.

"To the end that my glory may sing praise to Thee and not be silent." (Psalm 30:12)

We begin our course of sanctification when we first become believers, but we don't finish it until we are sanctified completely–body, soul and spirit–which usually takes a lifetime. Sanctification is really just a restructuring of our soul in conformity to Christ. Psalm 17:15 sums it up, "As for me, I will behold Thy face in righteousness: I shall be satisfied, when I awake, *with Thy likeness.*"

*Sanctification includes the process of separating the soulish things in our lives from the spiritual.* God is the only One who can do this, because He is the only One who truly knows *what is spiritual* and *what is soulish.* (John 2:25) We could never accomplish this separation in our own strength or by our own wisdom. Only God can do it by His Word! "For the Word of God is quick, and powerful, and sharper than any two-edged sword, <u>piercing</u> even to the *dividing asunder of soul and spirit, and of the joints and marrow,* and is a discerner of the thoughts and intents of the heart." (Hebrews 4:12)

Therefore, God is the One who separates, divides and <u>cuts away</u> anything in our souls that is not of the spirit and, instead, <u>carves</u> His own image. And, again, He often does this through suffering. The end result that He is after in each of our lives is that we might glorify, reflect and manifest His character to others and not our own.

A few months ago I was chatting with a friend on the phone and the conversation got around to the pain of becoming older. Without thinking, I said: "I really believe that if we are Christians and truly walking by the Spirit, then *our souls will never age.*" What I meant was, if we truly are living for the Lord, then our souls will be constantly be in a state of transformation. They won't grow old, but will simply mature in the Lord. Our physical bodies are what age, not our souls.

How often we hear people say, "Well, I really don't feel 60 (or 70 or 80). I feel just like I did 20 years ago." That's our soul speaking. However, if we <u>don't</u> have the Spirit of God dwelling in us, our soul will be heavily influenced by the aging of our bodies and most likely, will reflect a very different and very fleshly attitude. How often we *do* see that negativity in older people.

Sanctification simply means, "being made one" with Jesus so that the disposition that ruled Him can also rule and reign in us.

## The Big Question

The question we must ask ourselves is: Are we really willing to make the appropriate choices to deny ourselves, put off our sin and self and be sanctified body, soul and spirit? Are we willing to be conformed to His death? Are we really prepared for all that means?

A dear friend of mine, who used to be a missionary in New Zealand, wrote me a very provocative letter about this very subject:

"I read 1 Thessalonians 5:23 in my daily devotions this morning and it really spoke to my heart. 'And the very God of peace sanctify you wholly; and I pray God your whole spirit and soul and body be preserved blameless unto the coming of our Lord Jesus Christ.'

"When I read this, I had to ask myself: Am I really prepared to face the standard of these verses? We all take the term 'sanctification' much too lightly. Am I really prepared for what sanctification will cost me? *It will cost an intense narrowing of all my interests on earth, and an immense broadening of all my interests in God.*

"Sanctification means an intense concentration on God's point of view. It means every power of our body, soul and spirit must be chained and kept for God's purposes only. Am I prepared for God to do that in my life? Am I prepared to separate myself to God, even as Jesus did?"

These are good questions and ones that you might ask yourself. Are you prepared for what it will cost you? Because it will cost you everything that is not of God!

---

This chapter hopefully helps to clarify the criticalness of our moment-by-moment faith choices. They are the key to following the leading of the Spirit. Faith choices are the only avenue to being cleansed by the Spirit, to worshiping in the Spirit, to abiding in the Spirit and to walking in the Spirit–reflecting Him in all we do.

# Chapter Four Questions

1) What exactly is our new willpower?


2) Explain the two parts of our willpower.
   (2 Corinthians 8:11)


3) When we don't "feel" our choices, are they still
   genuine? (Philippians 2:13; 1 Corinthians 7:37;
   Matthew 26:39)


4) Do non-believers have this kind of willpower?
   Can they choose to go against how they
   feel and what they think?  Why?/ Why not?


5) As a result of our making faith choices or
   non-feeling choices, what two specific things
   will God do?


6) What then is the definition of "faith"?

7) Why is our moment-by-moment choice the key to life?

8) The character of our Christian life is determined by _____? Why?

9) What, then, is real Christian maturity?

10) Matthew 16:24 talks about "denying ourselves." What does this really mean?

11) When we choose to bar ourselves from following what we want, feel and desire, we often suffer. Why? (James 1:2-4)

12) What are some of the purposes for suffering? (Deuteronomy 8:2)

13) What does "sanctification" really mean? (1 Thessalonians 4:3,7; 5:23)

# Warfare Prayer

Dearest Lord: I desire to be a reflection of Your image so that my family, friends and others will see You in me and want what I have. Therefore, I choose to give You anything in me that would prevent my hearing directly from Your Spirit. I present my body as a living sacrifice, holy, acceptable unto You, which is my reasonable service. And I choose *not* to be conformed to this world but to be transformed (into Your image) by the renewing of my mind that I may prove what is Your good, acceptable and perfect will. (Romans 12:1-2)

I choose to "put on" the whole armor of God that I might be able to stand against the wiles of the enemy, having done all to stand strong. First of all, I choose to stand by having my loins girt about with truth and having on the breastplate of righteousness and Love guarding my heart. Next, I choose to shod my feet with the preparation of the Gospel of peace. Above all, I take up the shield of faith by which I can quench all the fiery darts of the enemy. Finally, ***I put on the helmet of salvation.*** (Ephesians 6:13-17)

# Chapter Five
## How to be Cleansed by the Spirit

So far, we've learned that glorifying the Lord–reflecting His Image–is the goal and purpose of all Christians. In order to do this, however, there are a couple of important things we must do: learn to love God by continually laying our wills and lives down to Him and learn how to make faith choices to do His will, regardless of what we think or feel. The result is that we'll be able to give God an open and cleansed vessel through which He can manifest or show forth Himself.

In this chapter, we want to concentrate on the specific steps necessary to cleansing ourselves so the Lord *can* use us. This is the practical application of "putting off" our sin and "putting on" Christ.

You might ask, "Why spend a whole chapter on this? Why make such a big deal out of this? Can't we just make one choice in the morning and, then, stay clean all day?"

For those of us who have tried to do this–make one choice in the morning and stay clean all day–the answer is a resounding "No." One choice in the morning to love God will *not* assure us of cleanliness all daylong!

If we are honest with ourselves, yielding ourselves completely to the Lord means, among other things, taking every thought captive and recognizing the ones that are not of Him. This is hard and takes time. And thus, is one of the reasons why much of the Christian Body is not interested in the moment-by-moment walk. Nonetheless, without separation from the sin and self that quench God's Spirit in us, we'll never be set free. <u>Jesus</u> is the One who exposes our sin; He is also the One who examines us, who cleanses us and who washes us from all the impurities. This is an on-going process every moment of the day, all day long!

## "Putting Off" And "Putting On"

The Scripture detailing this cleansing process is Ephesians 4:22-24, 31, which instructs us to *put off* the old man, which is corrupt according to the deceitful lusts, and be renewed in the spirit of your mind; and that ye *put on* the new man, which after God is created in righteousness and true holiness."[23]

What does it really mean to "put off the old man, be renewed in the spirit of your mind and put on the new man"? It means we must confess and repent of all the thoughts, emotions and actions in our lives that are <u>not</u> of God, give them to Him, and then watch as the Spirit of the Lord comes forth from our hearts.

---

[23]     Colossians 3:8-10, 12-16

Psalm 51 tells us the same thing but in a different way: "Wash me thoroughly from mine iniquity, and cleanse me from my sin. For I acknowledge my transgressions: and my sin is ever before me.... Purge me with hyssop, and I shall be clean: wash me, and I shall be whiter than snow."(verses 2- 3,7).[24]

Therefore, inner cleansing is essential. It's one of the major steps towards intimacy with Christ and being able to glorify Him in all we do. *Purification has always been a pre-requisite to being able to enter God's presence.* "Who shall ascend into the hill of the Lord? Or who shall stand in His Holy Place? He who hath <u>clean hands,</u> and <u>a pure heart</u>, who hath not lifted up his soul unto vanity, nor sworn deceitfully." (Psalm 24:3-4)

The practical application of just how we "cleanse our hands" and "develop a pure heart" can be patterned after the three steps the priests took in the Inner Court of Solomon's Temple in order to deal with their sin and be reconciled to God. Remember, Jesus tells us that everything in the Bible is there for our learning, for our understanding, and to be applied personally to our own lives. So here again, even in this cleansing service of the temple, there is a pattern that the Lord has laid out for us in order to deal with our sin and self, be reconciled to God and ultimately allowed to enter His presence.

---

[24]        See also Psalms 32

# Cleansing In the Temple

The Old Testament very often stressed the difference between the holy and the profane. For example, in Leviticus 11:44-45 it says, "For I am the Lord your God; ye shall therefore sanctify yourselves, and ye shall be holy; for I am holy."[25]   God is determined that His people understand exactly how to be totally consecrated to Him.

As we said, Solomon's Temple was designed to be God's special dwelling place and to reveal His glory to the world. (1 Kings 8) The Temple was a foreshadowing of the temple that was to come–Jesus Himself. However, Solomon's temple was filled with God's Glory *only after* the priests cleansed themselves in the Inner Court, worshiped in the Holy Place and came out to minister to the people. 2 Chronicles 5:11-14 tells us that "it came to pass, *when the priests were come out of the Holy Place*: (for all the priests that were present were sanctified...) And it came even to pass, as the trumpeters and singers were as one, to make one sound to be heard in praising and thanking the Lord...*then the house was filled with a cloud*, even the house of the Lord.  So that the priests could not stand to minister by reason of the cloud: for the glory of the Lord had filled the house."

This is the Lord's pattern for us also.

---

25      See also Leviticus 19:2; 20:26

What were the exact steps that the priests took in the Inner Court in order to be sanctified? There were three. Upon entering the Court, the priests first encountered *the Lavers*, where they washed their hands and feet by confessing and repenting of their sins. (Exodus 30: 19-21) Then they proceeded to *the Brazen Altar* where they gave their sin offerings to the Lord. Finally, they bathed bodily in *the Molten Sea,* which symbolized their complete washing and cleansing. These are the same three cleansing steps that I believe God wants us to implement in our own lives. He wants us to cleanse ourselves from "the filthiness of flesh and spirit" so we too, might have clean hands, a pure heart and are able to enter His presence and reflect His glory.

"Having therefore these promises, dearly beloved, let us cleanse ourselves from all *filthiness of the flesh and spirit*, perfecting holiness in the fear of God." (2 Corinthians 7:1) See also Psalm 15:1-2.

What we are about to learn then is *not* something I've made up or something that I've read in a self-help psychology book, but these are the actual steps that the priests took in Solomon's Temple in order to approach the Holy Place where they would worship Him.

# We Must be Believers

Before we go through these steps, however, it's very important to understand that unless we have asked Jesus Christ into our hearts to be our Savior and have been *born again* by His Spirit, these steps will <u>not</u> work. The Bible tells us that **without Christ's blood there is no remission of sin nor access to His presence.** And so, in order for this cleansing process to work, we must *first* have a brand-new spirit (or power source or life source) within us that *will* produce something different from what we naturally think, feel or want to do. We need the Holy Spirit in our hearts in order for there to be a true cleansing and change of heart. "Except a man be born of water and of the Spirit, he cannot enter into the kingdom of God. That which is born of the flesh is flesh; and that which is born of the Spirit is spirit." (John 3:5-6)

Therefore, a true Christian is one who has the Spirit of God dwelling in his heart, giving him *God's* authority and power to override his negative thoughts and feelings and to choose the Father's will, not his own. (Matthew 26:39) God, then, in His timing and way, will not only align this person's feelings with what he has chosen by faith, He will also give him the supernatural power to perform God's will in his life.

# Personal Cleansing Steps

In order to enter God's presence, we must not only be "believers" with the Spirit of God in our hearts, we must also be *clean*. Even if we are true believing Christians, we cannot just walk into the Holy Place any time we feel like it. God is holy and will commune with us only when we, too, are holy. He cannot abide where there is any corruption, sin or self. Thus, in order to enter His presence and worship Him as He desires, we must first *put off* any sin and self and *put on* Christ.

The following is a brief overview of the three specific cleansing steps required to cleanse our hearts so that God's Life can come forth. (If you want an in-depth explanation of how these steps work, I would really recommend taking a look at our textbook *Be ye Transformed*.)

**1)** The first step we must take in order to be a cleansed vessel is to **recognize and acknowledge any negative thoughts or emotions that have occurred**. It's important to "take these thoughts captive" as 2 Corinthians 10:5 tells us, look at them and allow God to give us His discernment about them. We must not *vent* these things nor *push them down* into the hidden part of our soul, but simply ask the Lord to expose what's *really* going on.

This is what the priests did at the Lavers of Bronze. The lavers themselves were made of women's looking glass (mirrors of polished metal). Thus, as the priests bent over the lavers to wash their hands, what they actually saw was their own reflection in the mirrored lavers. The priest's actions are symbolic of what the Lord requires us to do. We are to ask Him not only to expose what's going on in our *conscious thoughts and emotions*—the surface things that we <u>can</u> see–but we must also ask Him to shed light on the *buried things* in our soul, the root causes that we <u>cannot</u> see.

Our surface emotions are often just the *symptoms* of a much deeper cause. If the real root problem can be exposed, and subsequently gotten rid of, then the surface emotions will not occur again either. However, if we only deal with the external emotions and never the root causes, the surface problems will continue to come back. Therefore, it's essential that we always ask the Lord to expose any hidden root issues.

So whenever we find ourselves hurt, angry, resentful, envious, critical, self-centered, prideful, ungrateful, anxious, afraid, confused, bitter, judgmental or filled with any ungodly emotion, we must stop, get alone with the Lord and go through these steps. Ask the Lord to expose what is really going on. He is the only One who can cleanse our sin. And also the only One who can take those things from us "as far as the east is from the west" and completely heal us.

## "Fear Not the Original Thought"

In all my books and classes, I teach that "thoughts" are the most important ingredient of our makeup. This is where the battle is waged. The reason these are so important is that they are the first to be triggered in the chain reaction of our soul: our thoughts spark our emotions; our emotions cause our desires or our choices; and our choices determine whose life will be lived in our souls. This is why God tells us to first "take every thought captive." (2 Corinthian 10:5)

It's important to also understand that our first, original negative thought *is not sin.* It's what we choose to do with that negative thought that makes it sin or not. If we immediately recognize it and give it over to the Lord, we have not sinned and His Life can continue to flow. If, however, we mull that negative thought over and over again in our minds, we will need to confess it and repent of it, as it *has* already quenched God's Spirit in us.

One gentleman, who read *Be Ye Transformed* and was greatly touched by it, wrote this poem called "Fear not the Original Thought." It's a very long poem and thus I'm not able to include the entire poem here. (If you want to read all of it, we have it on our web site.) www.kingshighway.org/Fear_Not_the_Original_Thought.html

Here's the part that ministered to me:

"I used to feel so guilty and ashamed of the thoughts
That came into my mind.
How could a Godly man have such vain,
jealous, unclean thoughts?
How could a spirit-filled Christian think
so many un-Christ like things?
Was I really born again?

I asked God, "How could this be?"...

[*In answer to these questions,
God ministered these words to his heart.*]

"Fear not the original thought.
To have had it is not to have sinned.
But carefully discern the source of each thought.
Search for God's voice in the din.

"When a thought awakens emotion
And the emotion stirs your desire,
Don't act on the thought before measuring the cost
Of acting before you inquire.

"Who authored this thought?  And who will I please
If I bring this thought to life?
When the thought becomes act and I can't take it back
Am I closer to the Dark or the Light?"

Written by Terry Wetzsteon (9/2005)

**2)** The second essential step is that we must now **confess and repent of all that the Holy Spirit has shown us** and, in addition, **unconditionally forgive** anyone who has wronged us.

(This step is really part of step #1. But because so much goes on here, I've taken the liberty to separate it into two steps.)

*Confession* simply means, "owning" our sin and acknowledging that what we have done, either ignorantly or knowingly, has quenched God's Spirit in us. It's sin, therefore we must confess "ownership" of it. My Hebrew Bible translates confession as *spreading our hands*. In other words, we must come clean and confess all.

*Repenting*, then, means choosing to turn around from following what those negative thoughts and emotions are telling us and, instead, choosing to follow what God wants. This critical step of confession and repentance is our *own responsibility*. As 1 John 1:9 says, "If *we* confess our sins, [then] *He* is faithful and just to forgive us our sins."

This is the step, however, that many of us seem to leave out when we "give things over" to the Lord. Certainly, we acknowledge our hurts, fears and doubts to Him, but often we forget to admit our own responsibility in the situation. This is why so many of the things we've given to the Lord, often come back. If we *don't* do our part by confessing and repenting of them, God is hindered from doing His—taking them away.  (Psalm 103:12)

"I *acknowledged* my sin unto Thee, and mine iniquity have I not hid...I will *confess* my transgressions unto the Lord; and *Thou forgavest the iniquity of my sin.*" (Psalm 32:5)

Part of this second step of confession and repentance is that we must also **unconditionally forgive** others for whatever ill they have done to us.  Unforgiveness is one of the many things that quench God's Spirit in us and block His Life from coming forth.  Unforgiveness hinders God from working *in* us and *through* us.  Therefore, the way we release God to change our situations is by unconditionally forgiving the other party, *whether or not he has asked for it!*

Now, don't misunderstand me, we are *not* pardoning these people by doing this.  We don't have the authority to do that.  That's God's responsibility.  He is the judge. When we unconditionally forgive others, we are simply releasing them to Him, so that He can judge them righteously, and also *so that our response to their sin won't become a stumbling block in us*.

"For if ye forgive men their trespasses, your heavenly Father will also forgive you: But if ye forgive not men their trespasses, neither will your Father forgive your trespasses." (Matthew 6:14-15)

Both of the above steps (#1 & #2) occur at the Lavers of Bronze.

**3)** Once God has revealed our ungodly thoughts and emotions and we have confessed our responsibility in them, the third essential step is that we must **give everything that is not of faith over to Him.** God will not violate our free will by forcibly taking these things from us; we must willingly sacrifice and choose to hand them over to Him. This is the "putting off" that Ephesians talks about.

Romans 12:1 tells us that God wants us to give to Him—to sacrifice to Him, everything in us that is not of faith, so that it can be purged and cleansed by His blood. This is exactly what the priests did at the Brazen Altar as they sacrificed their offerings to the Lord. 2 Chronicles 7:1 gives us a vivid picture of just what happened: "Now when Solomon had made an end to praying, the fire came down from heaven and consumed the burnt offering and the sacrifices; and the glory of the Lord filled the house."

Being a *living sacrifice* means offering God the best of what we have to offer—ourselves! His Word tells us that offerings like this rise to Him as sweet smelling savor. (Exodus 29:18, 25) This sweet savor was the difference between Cain and Abel's offering. Abel followed God's instructions and his sweet smelling sacrifice was accepted.  Cain, on the other hand, didn't obey God's prescribed order and, thus, his offering was rejected.  It had no sweet aroma.

Most of the things that we give to the Lord are "of the flesh" and we'll *feel* them gone in a few days, if we are faithful to go through these three cleansing steps.  Psalm 103:12 tells us that when we give Him our sin, He promises to take it, "as far as the east is from the west."  However, some of the things that the Lord might expose could be long-standing strongholds of the enemy who won't let these kinds of things go easily.  So don't be dismayed if certain thoughts and feelings seem to reappear even after you have given them to God.

The truth is that the Lord takes our sin the moment we give it to Him, but often *our feelings don't align with those choices for a while.*  And this is where Satan tries to make us think that God is not faithful and that He has not cleansed us. Satan uses these "in-between" times—between the time we choose to give ourselves to God and the time the Lord finally aligns our feelings with our choices—to try to destroy us. <u>God</u>, on the other hand, lets us go as long as He knows is wise, to test us and to strengthen our faith. The question He is constantly asking us is: "Will you trust Me?  Will you trust Me in spite of what you feel or think or see?"

This is the step where the priests sacrificed their offerings on the Brazen Altar.

**4)** The fourth essential step in dealing with our sin and self is that we must **read God's Word and replace the lies with His Truth.** We must remember that God is the only One who can *cleanse, sanctify and heal our souls* completely by His Word.

Remember, it was at the Molten Sea—a huge bathtub that held thousands of baths—where the priests immersed themselves bodily in order to receive a total cleansing. At the Brazen Altar they had become all blood-splattered while sacrificing their offerings. Now they needed a complete bodily bathing in order to be thoroughly cleansed.

In like manner, after we have confessed, repented and given all to the Lord, we too are "bloody" and "torn apart" and in desperate need of God's complete healing power. Only reading or reciting Scriptures from the Word of God can totally restore us at this point. Only the Lord can wash us "with the washing of water by the Word." (Ephesians 5:26)

It's very helpful to memorize appropriate Scriptures for this particular step, so that if we are away from our Bibles, we can still put the Word of God back down in our innermost part where the lies have been. Scriptures like Psalm 32:5: "I have acknowledged my sin unto Thee, and mine iniquity have I not hid...I have confessed my transgressions unto the Lord; and Thou forgavest the iniquity of my sin." All of Psalm 51 is good. Also 1 John 1:5-10, Galatians 2:20 and 2 Corinthians 7:1 are wonderful Scriptures to remember.

After we have gone through all four of these steps: recognized and acknowledged our sins, confessed and repented of them, given them over to God and read His Word, we can be confident that He will cleanse us, align our feelings with our faith choices and perform His will through us.

At this point, having *put off* our sin and self, our body is cleansed and our spirit purified, and we have *put on* the "beauty of Christ's own holiness."[26] Just like the priests, we have changed our clothes and can now boldly enter the Lord's presence and worship Him.

   **CHART 7** is what we look like at this moment. (Page 104)

## The Need to be Clean

An important reminder here: In order to respond the way God would have us in a difficult situation, we must be cleansed. In other words, we must *never* confront someone unless we are a cleansed vessel. If we are not clean, it will be the "flesh" working, not the spirit, and the encounter will go poorly. Believe me, I know. I've tried it a hundred times the wrong way and it always back fires! *"Self," no matter how polished it is, does <u>not</u>*

---

[26]       Psalm 96:7-9; Psalm 29:2

*accomplish a thing!* The other party will immediately sense our judgmental attitude, react from his defenses, the truth will be hidden, and we'll sink even deeper into the pit than we were before.

If we can get clean first, then we can respond from God's Love and His Wisdom. The other person will sense our unconditional acceptance, respond from his heart and the situation will have a chance to turn around. (James 4:8)

## Right Choice/Wrong Life

I'm in the middle of reading a brand new book that just came out by a very popular and well-known speaker and author. It's a book on relationships, which, of course, is my heart's passion.

This gentleman begins by saying that after many years of teaching, writing and counseling, God has absolutely changed his life with some new insights. These new truths are that *you can choose your own reactions* and that those reactions are based on your thoughts. In brief, he is saying that your actions come from your thoughts. In other words, your thoughts are the basis for your feelings and your reactions. Thus, he stresses that we always have a choice as to how we will react.[27]

---

[27]      DNA Book, Gary Smalley, page 65

Well, he is absolutely right.  Our reactions <u>do</u> come from our thoughts!  However, if we don't know <u>how</u> to renew our minds (i.e., cleanse the grease from our heart), then *self* will come forth, *even if we have made the correct choices.*  Without cleansing, our response will always be the flesh, no matter what we choose.  *Thus, we must not only make the right choice, we must also cleanse our hearts, in order for our reaction to be "of God" and not of the flesh.*  Suffice to say, the grease has to be removed in order for God's Spirit to come forth.  As we empty out the flesh nature, we can then fill up with the Spirit.

Matthew 23:25-26 validates this, "Woe unto you, scribes and Pharisees, hypocrites! *For ye make clean the outside of the cup and of the platter, but within they are full of extortion and excess.*  Thou blind Pharisee, *cleanse first that which is within the cup and platter, that the outside of them may be clean also.*"

God's Life can only be shown forth *after* we have confessed, repented and given our self-life over to the Lord.

God's Spirit is what changes us.  There's nothing we can do in our own power and strength to implement this change.  It all must be done by His Spirit *in* us and His Life *through* us.  Paul confirms this when he says, "Why look ye so earnestly on us, as though *by our own power* or holiness we had made this man walk?" (Acts 3:12)

# Evidence of Renewal

Once we have been cleansed and renewed from the inside out, there are three things that will begin to manifest themselves in our lives: *freedom, Love and trust.*

One of the first evidences that we are, indeed, beginning to be renewed in the spirit is **freedom**. This is freedom from sin and self-controlling us. It's the freedom to be ourselves with no hypocrisy and no phoniness. It's the freedom to fail and yet know that as we ask God's forgiveness, He will be there to restore us. It's also the freedom to forgive others when they sin against us, knowing that, but for the grace of God, go I. Nothing in all the world compares to this freedom of life.

The next evidence of renewal in spirit is **Love**. This is God's Love in our hearts, which is now able to freely flow out into our lives. It's not the love of the world, but the Love of Jesus enabling us not only to totally give ourselves over to Him, but also enabling us to unconditionally love those who have despitefully used us. John 13:35 tells us that "by this shall all men know that ye are my disciples, *if ye have love one to another.*"

And, of course, the last evidence that we have been renewed in the spirit of our minds is the ability to **trust** the Lord *in all circumstances.* Trusting the Father in the good times is easy, but trusting Him in the "night seasons," through tragedies and death, is difficult at best.

The ability to trust Him fully in these times is evidence that we are, indeed, on the path to transformation.

## Erica's Example

Erica is the young 29-year-old woman who gave such incredible and powerful testimony about *overcoming* in Chapter Two.   In that chapter, she told us about her struggles and the experiences she had against the powers of darkness that war around each of us; she told us how she began to experience the Love of God in her life and how her life dramatically began to change; and how she is now willing to be used in whatever way the Lord desires.

I asked her about these three evidences of renewal *freedom, love and trust*.   Here, again, is what she had to say:

"For 15 years I walked around full of anger, bitterness and hopelessness.  I was controlled by these emotions and became a very unlikable person.  The drug life-style that I was in was something I never thought I could be free of. Unless, of course, I died. Which as you know, I tried to do numerous times.

In fact, three weeks before I finally gave my heart and life to Christ, I was in a serious car wreck (a D.U.I. that was totally my fault).  But, because I didn't actually die in that crash, the next day at the Trauma Center, I intentionally overdosed again trying to take my own life. God, however, knew, *even back then*, that *HE* was going to set me free. And, three weeks later, when I did ask Him to take over my life, He again promised me that freedom. Since that day, I have and I am experiencing just that–freedom from all the hurt and pain I caused others and freedom from all the things that others did to me. Nothing in the world can compare to this freedom of spirit.

I have been hurt physically, emotionally and sexually in so many ways. But, I now have a loving Father in Heaven who has told me that He will *never* hurt me. I can trust Him because He truly loves me and will never break His promises. He has been so faithful to even show me how all of His promises about me have come true. Not one of them has been broken. He loves me even when I disappoint Him or let Him down. He showed me that He has always been there; I just never reached up and grabbed a hold of His hand. Knowing He loves me so much and forgives me of everything has allowed me to not only give that unconditional Love out to others, but to trust Him in all things.

My life is, indeed, rich and full. Far richer than I ever could have imagined when I was running around as a lost, lonely and hopeless person. It only changed because God took the initiative and reached out to me. *He found me!* I began with a faith choice to believe in

Him and I am learning to live by faith, putting everything in my life into His hands, asking that only His will be done, not my own.

———————————

So, just like everything else, it's impossible to glorify the Lord unless we are, first of all, cleansed by the Lord. Then, the "beauty of the Lord" can come forth. Renewal is essential to being a mirror that reflects every detail of Christ's character to the world.

These are the steps to moment-by-moment cleansing our temple so that we can "worship in the Spirit," "abide in the Spirit" and "walk in the Spirit." Thus, glorifying Him.

# Chapter Five Questions

1) We learned earlier that God desires us to *put off* the old man and to *put on* the new. What does this mean practically? (Ephesians 4:22-32; 2 Corinthians 7:1; Colossians 3:8-10)

2) What are the actual steps to putting off our sin and self?  And what is the Scriptural basis for these? (Leviticus 9:2; 2 Chronicles 5:11-14; Psalm 51:2-3, 7)

3) In order for these steps to work, what is the basic requirement? (John 3:5-6)

4) What is the first step in putting off the old man and what does it mean in practical terms? (2 Corinthians 10:5)

5) What is the next step that we must do? (1 John 1:9; Psalm 32:5; Matthew 6:14-15)

6) Once God has revealed our ungodly thoughts and emotions to us, and we have forgiven (or released) others involved, what must we do next? (Romans 12:1)


7) Why do some of the things we give to the Lord seem to reappear again?


8) The fourth step in giving things to the Lord is to read His Word and replace the lies with the truth. What does this mean in practical terms?


9) Why is cleansing so important to the Lord? (Hebrews 12:14; James 4:8; Matthew 23:25-26)


10) What are the three evidences of renewal?

# Warfare Prayer

Dearest Lord: I desire to be a reflection of Your image so that my family, friends and others will see You in me and want what I have. Therefore, I choose to give You anything in me that would prevent my hearing directly from Your Spirit. I present my body as a living sacrifice, holy, acceptable unto You, which is my reasonable service. And I choose *not* to be conformed to this world but to be transformed (into Your image) by the renewing of my mind that I may prove what is Your good, acceptable and perfect will. (Romans 12:1-2)

I choose to "put on" the whole armor of God that I might be able to stand against the wiles of the enemy, having done all to stand strong. First of all, I choose to stand by having my loins girt about with truth and having on the breastplate of righteousness and Love guarding my heart. Next, I choose to shod my feet with the preparation of the Gospel of peace. Above all, I take up the shield of faith by which I can quench all the fiery darts of the enemy. Finally, *I put on the helmet of salvation and the sword of the Spirit, which is the Word of God*. (Ephesians 6:13-17)

# Chapter Six
## How to Worship in the Spirit

My main purpose for writing this book is to try and describe the goal of the Christian life. As we have seen, it's certainly not head knowledge, nor self-confidence or self-esteem, but choosing moment-by-moment to lay our wills and lives down so that Jesus can be glorified through us.

In Chapter Two, we explored the war that is continually fought between God's Spirit in our hearts and the sin and self that reside in our soul and body. We found that the *key* to winning this war is learning how to make faith choices to "put off" the flesh and "put on" Christ. As we do this on a daily basis, we'll be able to enter God's presence and worship Him. As mentioned before, *worship is the step that ultimately leads to glorifying Him.*

*Worship, however, is always contingent upon cleansing (as we saw in the temple model).* Listen to Psalm 24:3-4, "Who shall ascend into the hill of the Lord [to worship Him]? Or who shall stand in His holy place? He who hath *clean hands*, and *a pure heart*, who hath not lifted up his soul unto vanity, nor sworn deceitfully." The Lord is saying here that it's our heart that determines whether or not we are able to truly worship. If our heart is cleansed and God's Spirit able to come forth, then we'll be able to enter His presence and commune with Him. If our heart is covered with grease (as Psalm 119:70 describes) and God's Spirit quenched by sin or self, then our worship will be an empty religious act, not changing us at all nor impressing anyone else, least of all the Lord.

In his recent Pulpit Series newsletter, Pastor Wilkerson said:

"...a Christian can pray diligently without ever really worshipping. Indeed, it's possible to be a prayer warrior and intercessor and still not be a worshipper of God. You can plead for your unsaved children, pray for the needs of an entire church, be holy and meek in seeking God's burden–and yet never truly worship Him!

"...in short, worship cannot be learned! It's a spontaneous outbreak–the act of a heart that's been overwhelmed by a revelation of God's glory and His incredible Love for us."[28]

## Worship in the Temple

Let's explore the worship services in Solomon's Temple again, and see what parallels might stand out. What was the *order of service* for the priests?

First, the priests came into the Outer Courts where they praised and thanked God. Next, they cleansed

---

[28]    David Wilkerson, *Times Square Church Pulpit Series,*
       "The Effects of Seeing the Glory of God."

themselves (the four steps) in the Inner Court. Then, they entered God's presence and worshiped Him in the Holy Place. And finally, they were able to glorify the Lord by demonstrating all that the Lord had given them in the sanctuary. Note that they glorified the Lord *only after* they had praised Him, *only after* they had cleansed themselves and *only after* they had worshiped Him in the Holy Place.

In like manner, we will be able to glorify the Lord only *after* we have praised Him, only *after* we have cleansed ourselves and only *after* we have worshiped Him in the "beauty of holiness." (Psalm 29:2) The Bible speaks of the "beauty of holiness" as something that happens *after* we have been purified, body and soul. At that point, sin has been dealt with and self has been set aside, so the beauty of Christ's holiness can come forth. This is the point at which we can boldly enter God's presence and worship Him in the same nature as He–in the spirit.

The New Testament book of Hebrews validates this, "Having therefore, brethren, boldness to enter into the holiest by the blood of Jesus, by a new and living way, which He hath consecrated for us, through the veil, that is to say, His flesh. And having an high priest over the house of God, let us draw near with a true heart in full assurance of faith, having our hearts sprinkled from an evil conscience, and our bodies washed with pure water." (10:19-22)

# Definition of Worship

The Greek word for worship in the New Testament is *proskuneo* (which actually means to kiss). It's the same word used for a dog licking his master's feet. Worship means to prostrate oneself in homage, to bow down the self and to exalt God. It's the submission of our entire being to God. Worship then is the union of our spirits with God's Spirit in the Holy Place of our hearts. (Romans 8:26)

Worship means to ascribe worth to a being or object. In other words, whatever we value or place the highest worth on is what we worship. Interestingly enough, the attributes of the gods we worship eventually seem to manifest their characteristics in us. Rather than Christ's image being carved into the walls of our soul, these ungodly characteristics are inscribed there. Psalm 135: 18 even tells us that we become *like* what we worship.

A great example of this is the country of Egypt. Egypt used to worship the scarab beetle, which is actually a dung beetle found in manure piles. If you visit Egypt today, you'll notice that the Nile riverbed is covered with dung and fecal material, as the cattle, animals and even children relieve themselves there. The countryside is filthy. Trash is everywhere. Egypt is also a country that is preoccupied with death (mummies, etc.). The whole country has become like what it has worshiped–it's a culture of death and decay and refuse.

We *do* become like what we worship! Our values, our priorities and how we live our lives revolve around what we commit ourselves to, which ultimately determines what flows from our lives. The bottom line is that the object of our worship is the guiding force in our lives.

If we want to become more Christ-like and begin to glorify the Lord more, we must learn to worship Him more. The changes in our inner being only occur when we are in the presence of the Lord. The Lord says in Exodus 25:22, "And there I will meet with thee, and I will commune with thee from above the mercy seat." And He promises to, "Show [us] the path of life: *In Thy presence is fulness of joy;* at Thy right hand there are pleasures for evermore." (Psalm 16:11)

This last verse is saying that in His presence, God will fill us with unspeakable joy and the strength to withstand any circumstance. (Nehemiah 8:10d) As a result, we'll be able to share His glory to an even greater degree.

## Why Worship is Important

Worship is important because it releases blessings in two directions: we come into the Lord's presence by loving and adoring Him; He, then, makes Himself known by communicating His Love back to us through revelation, insight and love. Worship, in other words, is a two-way communication. We worship the Lord; He then meets with us and changes us.

On a recent trip to Israel, we visited the Temple Institute in Jerusalem where the guide made an interesting statement. She said, "The priests worshiped the Lord in the Holy Place, specifically at the Incense Altar. It was here that they felt the *connection* was made between man and the Lord." I was so excited because so many of my books surmised this, but I had never actually heard it stated that way until this particular trip.

Worship is a two-way connection that occurs at the altar of our hearts. It consists of not only receiving God's Love, but also loving Him in return. Suffice to say that if we haven't *first* received His Love and surrendered ourselves to Him, we haven't really had communion with Him. Communion and worship are all about *mutual* affection–both giving and receiving. To love Him (*agapao*) demands that we reciprocate by loving Him with all our heart, mind and soul. The bottom line is that worship strips away "self" and allows God to conform us more into His image.

The key to worship, however, is that it can only be done "in the spirit" and not in the flesh. Just as Pastor Wilkerson said, we can spend hours a day in prayer telling the Lord how much we love Him, but if we still are in the flesh, we haven't really worshiped at all! It's only by the Spirit that we can apprehend God and it's only by the Spirit that we can honor, adore and glorify Him. God's Spirit is the only One who can re-create us in the likeness of Christ. John 4:24 tells us that since

God is a Spirit, those that worship Him must worship Him "in spirit and in truth." (Truth, here, simply means in sincerity and honesty.)

So, learning how to worship the Lord in spirit is critical.[29] And, it's <u>not</u> a once a week function, but should dominate our lives seven days a week. Sunday worship is meaningless, unless it is preceded by six days of cleansing, loving and communing with the Lord. Unless we are living a life of love, our worship will be empty.

As we said a little while ago, worship is important because Scripture tells us we become *like* what we worship. (Psalm 135:18) Thus, the more we worship the Lord, the more we will become changed into His likeness. When we restrict our worship to man's traditions, however, we'll never be changed. Only true worship will allow us to ultimately glorify Him.

## Seeing Ourselves as we Truly Are

Another benefit of worship is that it allows us to see ourselves as we truly are. When Isaiah and Job came into the Lord's presence, it exposed the truth about themselves. Isaiah tells us in Chapter 6, verse 5 that: "Woe is me! For I am undone; because I am a man of unclean lips." And Job tells us that he uttered these words when he entered the Lord's holy place, " Wherefore I abhor myself, and repent in dust and ashes." (Job 42:5-6)

---

29     1 Chronicles 16:29; Psalm 29:2; 95:6-9; Matthew 4:10; Philippians 3:3

Seeing ourselves as we truly are is essential. We must see the need for personal change; see the need to dedicate ourselves to Him in an even greater degree; see the need to lay our burdens at His feet and pray more; and finally, see the need to exalt Him in everything.

When we allow the Lord to personally change us as a result of our worship times, we'll be able to more adequately reflect Christ to others. We won't have to "say" anything. Our behavior alone will prove that we have been in the Lord's presence. When we truly live like this, we won't have to convince others that Christ is the answer, they will already have seen His character in us and *they will want what we have.* This type of Christianity would revolutionize the church.

Unfortunately, the opposite is also true. If our behavior doesn't reflect Christ or show forth His Love, we will push people farther away from the truth.

I went to lunch with a friend recently who was very needy. I asked a pastor friend of mine to also join us. The pastor didn't really want to come because he said he was "very busy," but he felt obligated and came anyway. That pastor *said* all the right things to my friend at lunch, but later when my friend called up to say "thank you," she shared privately, "That pastor didn't really want to be there with me, did he?" Truly, our life actions betray our words and often reveal the real truth. This encounter, rather than pushing my friend closer to the Lord, pushed her farther away from Him. *Glorifying Christ occurs when both our words and our actions validate each other.* When what we are saying confirms what we are doing. Unless our "life actions" bear witness with our "words," others will disregard our message, just like my friend did!

Worship is not only the *door* to intimacy with the Lord, it's also the *key* to His joy (Ps.16:11) and the *means* by which we receive His strength. (Nehemiah 8:10). Without these two things, we won't be able to withstand the trials that the Lord allows in our lives. Worship enables us to experience His joy and strength, no matter what troubles we face.

## Our Cultural Context Has Defined our Worship

We Americans live in a self-centered "fast food" society where we have drive-in churches, drive-through markets and quickie divorces. We want things handed to us on a silver plate, without doing any work ourselves or requiring any personal change. Our worship services are no different.

The motivation for many Christians today to worship is so that they might "enjoy themselves" and be entertained, not necessarily to honor God or be changed. Their focus is on themselves, not on God. Modern worship has become horizontal, rather than vertical.

**God never intended worship to be something to *engage* the audience, but something that would *change* the audience.**

Here's an interesting fact: There are more worship CDs being sold today than ever before. Yet, there are more Christian's lives, marriages and families falling apart. Something is terribly wrong. We are listening to worship music, but <u>not</u> becoming true worshipers. Genuine worship cannot be manufactured or produced by our fleshly efforts. In other words, no amount of music can produce it and no amount of planning can manufacture it. When we attempt to do so out of our fleshly abilities, we fool ourselves into thinking it's the real thing. But, in truth, it's not worship, it's a counterfeit. True worship begins in the heart and only succeeds when we truly enter God's presence.

## Jesus–A Whole New Way to Worship

God designed Solomon's Temple to be His special dwelling place, a place of worship and a place to reveal His glory. (1 Kings 8:1-21; Exodus 40:34-35) It was the place that He chose to put *His Name* forever. (1 Kings 9: 3) But, in the New Testament when the temple curtain was torn (Matthew 2:51), it symbolized the opening of a *new* way to worship. *Jesus* became the new temple (Matthew 12:6) where God now dwells and through which His Spirit moves and acts.[30] Jesus represents the new covenant.[31]

---

[30]     1 Corinthians 2:11-17; Ephesians 2:18-22; Matthew 12:18-21
[31]     Matthew1:22-23; Luke 22:20; 1 Corinthians11:25;
        Jeremiah 31:31-34; Mark 14:24

In other words, Jesus introduces us to a totally new way of relating to God. (John 4:23-24) No more are we required to worship in the physical temple. We are to worship through a Person and that Person is Christ. (John 17:3) He becomes the center of true worship. He is the fulfillment of everything in the old temple. He is the focus of worship in the New Testament and He is the *meeting place* that God has chosen to manifest His glory. Thus, a specific place or time of worship is not needed anymore because true worship is independent of place or ceremony.

1 Kings 8:27 confirms this, "Will God indeed dwell on the earth? Behold, the heaven and heaven of heavens cannot contain Thee; how much less this house that I have builded."

Jesus' worship of the Father culminated in His sacrificial death for us. Our faith, therefore, is best expressed when we offer ourselves back to the Lord as a living sacrifice. Then we are able to glorify Him both in body and spirit, which are His. (John 10:17; 1 Corinthians 6:20)

Again, see **CHART 7**, page 104.

## Sacrifice–the Heart of Worship

Sacrifice, therefore, is the heart of worship. Laying down all that *we* desire, all that *we* want and all that *we* feel, is what worship is all about. The heart of worship is the offering of our very lives and our very selves. When we worship we bring the gift of our self to the Lord to use, as He desires. (Psalms 96:8-9)

It's interesting because there were <u>two</u> compartments in Solomon's Temple. These, to me, represent the two stages of Christian life: *The Holy Place* symbolizes God's intimate presence–the place where we worship and become one with Him (this would be the "spiritual" Christian who is walking by the Spirit); and *the Inner Court* which symbolizes being saved but in desperate need of cleansing, worshiping and abiding (this would be the "carnal" Christian living in the Spirit only).

Worship is also the key to edification. (2 Chronicles 5:11-13) As we personally worship and love the Lord in our prayer closets, we are able to then go out and serve and glorify Him in the world. Oswald Chambers in his wonderful book *My Utmost for His Highest* says, "My worth to God in public is what I am in private."

Jack Hayford in his excellent book, *Worship His Majesty,* says that "Worship is what leads to His presence and being able to reflect Him in all we do. *Worship gets us from head knowledge to foot knowledge.* It's the bridge between being just His people and being a genuine example of His likeness." (Isaiah 40:5)

*After we have been worshiping in God's presence, we will carry His beauty and His holiness around with us.* And it will be obvious to all we meet that we have been with the Lord. Just as Moses's face shone after his meeting with the Lord on Mt. Sinai, so we'll reflect what we worship!

Exodus 34:29-35 tells us, "And it came to pass, when Moses came down from Mount Sinai with the two tables of testimony in Moses' hand, when he came down from the mount, that Moses knew not that *the skin of his face shone* while he talked with him. And when Aaron and all the children of Israel saw Moses, behold, *the skin of his face shone*; and they were afraid to come near him. And Moses called unto them and Aaron and all the rulers of the congregation returned unto him: and Moses talked with them. And afterward all the children of Israel came near: and he gave them in commandment all that the Lord had spoken with him in Mount Sinai. And till Moses had finished speaking with them, he put a veil on his face. But when Moses went in before the Lord to speak with Him, he took the veil off, until he came out. And he came out, and spoke unto the children of Israel that which he was commanded. And the children of Israel saw the face of Moses, that *the skin of Moses' face shone*: and Moses put the veil upon his face again, until he went in to speak with Him."

Thus, worshiping in the spirit is essential if we want to reflect Christ in all we do.  It's the means by which we are changed into Christ's image.  Acts 2:28 tells us that as a result of worship, the Lord will make us full of joy with His countenance.  Worship is that inner connection that translates into an outer manifestation of His glory.  (Should you want to explore this subject in greater depth, I would recommend reading *Private Worship: The Key to Joy*, the companion to this book.)

# **Chapter Six Questions**

1) Why is worship the step that ultimately leads
   to glorifying the Lord? (Psalms 24:3-4;
   Hebrews 10:19-22) And why is it so important?
   (Exodus 20:3)

2) Define what worship really means. (Romans 8:26;
   Luke 7:45; 1 Corinthians 14:25)

3) Is worship something we do *externally* or
   *internally*?  Explain your answer.

4) Worship releases blessings in two directions.
   What are they?

5) How do we become "like" what we worship?
   (Psalm 135:18)

6) What does it mean to worship in the Spirit?
   (John 4:24) Give an example in Scripture
   of a man or woman who did this. (Psalm 63:1-4;
   Matthew 26:6-13)

7) Worship allows us to see ourselves as we truly are. Why is this important? (Isaiah 6:5; Job 42:5-6)

6) What is the real *heart* of worship and why is it the "key" to edification? (Psalm 96:8-9; 2 Chronicles 5:11-13)

# Warfare Prayer

Dearest Lord: I desire to be a reflection of Your image so that my family, friends and others will see You in me and want what I have. Therefore, I choose to give You anything in me that would prevent my hearing directly from Your Spirit. I present my body as a living sacrifice, holy, acceptable unto You, which is my reasonable service. And I choose *not* to be conformed to this world but to be transformed (into Your image) by the renewing of my mind that I may prove what is Your good, acceptable and perfect will. (Romans 12:1-2)

I choose to "put on" the whole armor of God that I might be able to stand against the wiles of the enemy, having done all to stand strong. First of all, I choose to stand by having my loins girt about with truth and having on the breastplate of righteousness and Love guarding my heart. Next, I choose to shod my feet with the preparation of the Gospel of peace. Above all, I take up the shield of faith by which I can quench all the fiery darts of the enemy. Finally, I put on the helmet of salvation and the sword of the Spirit, which is the Word of God. (Ephesians 6:13-17) *Praying always and on every occasion in the power of the Holy Spirit, keeping alert and persistent in praying for Christians everywhere.* (Ephesians 6: 13-18)

# Chapter Seven
## How to Abide in the Spirit

Glorifying God is a subject that should dominate our lives. John 14:13 tells us that we are to make *His* glory the aim of everything we do. In short, our lives should continually reflect His person, His character and His Love and should cause others to look upon Him. In order to do this, however, we must live in, be led by and *abide in* God's Spirit. We must be controlled only by His Spirit and <u>not</u> be again entangled with the yoke of bondage (sin). We must stand fast and *abide in* the liberty that Christ has given us.

"And now, little children, *abide in Him;* that, when He shall appear, we may have confidence, and not be ashamed before Him at His coming." (1 John 2:28)

What does it mean to "abide in Him" or to "abide in the Spirit?" Abiding means *remaining in, staying in, dwelling in or continuing in the Holy Place.* It means staying in the Lord's presence. It means continuing to worship Him and be fruit bearers to others. Psalm 91 tells us that "He who *dwells* in the secret place of the most High *shall abide under the shadow of the Almighty.*" Simply speaking, this means the one who *dwells* in the Holy Place shall *abide* under His protection. It's a promise of deliverance, protection, safety and a long life to those who remain in His presence, Wow! The only requirement to attain this is: to make the Lord our habitation, to set our love upon Him and to know His Name." (vs.9 & 14) Suffice to say, if we *abide* in that place of worship and adoration, then all the above promises will be ours. If we quench His Spirit, however, and cease to wait, dwell or abide in the Holy Place, we will lose His protection, His deliverance and open ourselves up to the *snares* of the enemy and spiritual attacks of all kinds. Remember Pastor Bruce in Chapter One? He is a good example of this. For a brief moment, he forgot about God's ways and waited *not* for His counsel, which was the beginning of his spiral downward. (Psalm 106:13) He was ensnared by the enemy and then fell into his pit.

## Abiding in Christ

As we have shared before, there's a big difference between *being born of the Spirit* and *walking in the Spirit.* We are all born anew by the Spirit from the time we ask Christ to come into our lives and forgive us of our sins, but we only walk in the Spirit when we follow the Spirit's leading and bear fruit. Galatians 5:25 exhorts us, "*If we live in the Spirit, let us also walk in the Spirit.*" And Colossians 2:6 confirms this: "As you have received Christ, so [now] walk in Him."

Be aware that there is a subtle difference between *abiding in the Spirit* and *walking by the Spirit.* These two can almost be interchangeable, with one small exception.

Abiding means resting in, staying in, remaining in and waiting in God's presence, bearing the fruit of love, joy, peace, etc. Whereas as we will see next chapter, walking by the Spirit is taking that fruit and actually giving it out to the world. *It's doing, not just being*!

Ultimately, these two steps–abiding in the Spirit and walking in the Spirit–must go hand in hand. We can't give the fruit of the Spirit out to anyone if we are not *first* abiding in His presence to receive it.

John 15 is a wonderful chapter devoted to what it means to abide in God and bring forth fruit:

"In this is my Father glorified, that ye bear much fruit..." (John 15:8)

What is the *fruit* spoken of here? Galatians 5:22-23 tells us that this is the "fruit of the Spirit"–Love, joy, peace, longsuffering, gentleness, goodness, faith, meekness, temperance..." Fruit occurs when these attributes of Christ show up in our lives. Fruit is born when we begin to possess Christ-likeness and begin to pass that Love of Jesus on to others.

A dear friend of ours who is a Greek scholar, pointed out to me that the word *to bear* in John 15:2 could be translated "*to carry fruit from one location to another.*" In other words, to be an open channel passing along God's Life from the Father to others.

He also suggested that the phrase "abide in Me" or "remain in Me" could also be translated "*rest in My Love.*" Then God's promise to us in verse 7 makes much more sense. If we continue to "rest in His Love," then we can ask whatever we will, *consistent with bearing fruit*, and He will do it.

Here is my friend's translation of John 15:1-7:

"15:1: I [Jesus] am the true vine and my Father is the vine keeper. 2: He takes away each of My [Jesus'] branches that do not carry fruit, and He cleanses each [one] that does so that it may carry even more.

"3: You are already clean through the teaching that I have spoken to you. 4: Rest in my Love, and I will be with you. Just as the branch cannot carry fruit by itself [unless it remains on the vine], so neither can you [carry fruit], unless you rest in My Love.

"5: I am the vine; you are the branches. Whoever rests in My Love and lets My Love rest within him can carry lots of fruit, because without Me you cannot accomplish anything. 6: If anyone fails to rest in My Love, he shall be cast out like a [withered] branch, and they shall gather them and cast them into the fire, and the fire shall burn.

"7: If you rest in My Love, and my sayings take root within you, ask whatever you want to happen, and it shall come about for your benefit. 8: My Father is glorified [when you do this]–when you carry lots of fruit, you demonstrate that you have become my disciples."

## Vineyard Explanation

As long as we are talking about grapevines, fruit and branches, let's see if we can find any parallels to the Christian life. (God always has hidden meanings that are exciting to discover!)

Grape vines are unique. They tend to grow so vigorously that they often spread out in all different directions and do everything *but* bear fruit. In order to produce fruit, they must be pruned quite often. In the ancient vineyards, the vinedresser pruned the branches in two ways: he chopped off the dead wood that bred disease and insects, and he also cut away the living tissue so that the life of the vine would not be dissipated or the quality of the crop jeopardized. Sometimes the vinedresser would even cut away whole bunches of grapes so that the rest of the crop would be of a higher quality.

Well, Christians are very much like those grape vines. We tend to grow so vigorously that we often spread out in all different directions. And, just like those vines, we often have a lot of non-fruitful wood that must be cut away in order to produce fruit. In fact, sometimes we can become so dense in our external leaf productions (ministry, work, family, busyness, etc.) that the Son (like the sun) cannot reach into the area where fruit is supposed to form.  Left to ourselves, without the Lord's help, we'll tend to favor our own new expansion of territory rather than bear more fruit for Him.

What is the spiritual result of this?  From a distance our lives might look incredibly green and healthy, but the Lord knows us intimately and He knows that there's just a little harvest for Him.  Thus, just like the grape vine that must be pruned in order to produce more fruit, the Lord takes His shears to us.  Sometimes He cuts away the dead wood that prevents our growth, but more often He cuts away the living tissue that robs us of our spiritual vigor.  This, obviously, is extremely painful.

Sin is like the dirt that covers the grape leaves.  Air and light cannot get in and thus, the branch languishes and no fruit develops.  How does the vinedresser lift the dirt and mud?  The same way the Father deals with us.  Again, by more washing and pruning.[32]

"My son, despise not thou the chastening of the Lord, nor faint when thou are rebuked of Him.  For whom the Lord loveth He chasteneth, and scourgeth every son whom He receiveth.  If ye endure chastening, God dealeth with you as with sons; for what son is he whom the father chasteneth not?  But if ye be without chastisement, wherewith *all* are partakers, then are ye bastards, and not sons." (Hebrews 12:5b-8)

---

[32]     From "Jesus - I Am the Vine." www.discoverthebook.org

At the time, chastisement is painful. But, when a spiritual crop is produced, we can see the Lord's hand in all of it and be confident that He knew exactly what He was doing. The Lord's focus is always on the *quality* of the harvest, not just the *quantity*. He is glorified not only by a bigger crop, but by one that is also a better crop. The fruit we produce is not just to please ourselves, but to serve others.

## The Fruit of Love

"By this shall all men know that ye are my disciples, *if ye have love one to another.*" (John 13:35) This Scripture says it all. If we have Love (*Agape*), others will know we are Christians. If we don't, they won't. Without Love, Paul says, we are nothing! (1 Corinthians 13:2) In other words, we will be spiritually corrupt. Again, "carnal Christians."

Puritan John Owen once said: "One may be capable of performance that benefits others public ally and yet be a stranger himself to the Spirit-wrought inner transformation that true knowledge of God brings. The manifestation of the Spirit in Charismatic performance is not the same thing as the fruit of the spirit in Christ-like character. Christ-likeness is what matters."[33]

---

[33]      J.T. Packer, *Keep in Step with the Spirit,* page 30, Baker Books, 2005

So again the proof that we are, indeed, believers comes <u>not</u> through our knowledge of Scripture, from our spiritual gifts or by our church attendance, but only by showing God's Love and Life to others.

## Friends of God

John 15:14 goes on to tell us that if we are obedient and remain in His Love, carrying it to others, then we will be His "friends." Another beautiful Scripture that validates this relationship is Proverbs 22:11: "He that loveth [totally gives himself over to] pureness of heart...the King shall be his friend."

Abraham is a good example of one who rested in and remained in God's Love. And, he is remembered in Scripture as a "friend of God" and one who "walked with God." Abraham had that intimate relationship with the Lord that we all desire. Staying in, remaining in and resting in God's Love is the only way to achieve this union. Friendship with God means seeing Him "face to face."

The *key* here, again, is having a pure heart. Why? Because only then can God's Love flow freely and purely from our hearts out into our lives. Remember CHART 7. This is what it means to "stay in" God's Love, and this is what makes us His friends. Having His Love not only in our hearts, but also flowing from our lives is proof that we are, indeed, abiding in God.

As we look around us—at our churches, our families, our friends, and our kids—many have been caught up in the do's and don'ts of Scripture and ministries that seem to focus on one specialized area like: prophecy, gifts of the Spirit, witnessing, healing, miracles, faith, signs and wonders, etc. But, if we look closely at these movements, one must ask: *where's God's Love? How can we be Spirit-filled and yet not Love-filled?* Aren't they the very same thing? God's Love is the glue that ties us all together and what's so scary is that it's absent from many churches, ministries and believers these days. Matthew 24:12 gives us the simple Scriptural answer. Speaking about these end times, it says: "And because iniquity shall abound, the *Agape Love of many will grow cold.*" This Scripture is talking about us!

God's Love doesn't just fall out of heaven. His Love comes through us. *We are extensions of His Love* to one another. All He wants from us is a willing body—arms and legs—to pour His Love through.

Larry Crabb's book called *Inside Out* shares that Christians can spend years in Bible study developing a real love for the truth; but, if they come away *without* God's Love for people, then they will have wasted their entire time. *The whole purpose of Bible study is to make us more loving, not more scholarly.*

David Needham (*Birthright*) confirms this same thought, by saying: "the big task is <u>not</u> the finding of the truth, but the living of it!" This, to me, says it all!

It's only Jesus' Love through us that will bring our families, our husbands, our children, our neighbors, and our bosses to the feet of Jesus. Since God is Love, the only way these people will ever know that we are indeed Christians is by the *real* Love (fruit) they see and feel coming from us. Abiding in His presence is the only thing that produces this kind of Love.

1 Peter 4:8 urges us, "Above all things have fervent Love among yourselves; for Love shall cover the multitude of sins." This means that if true *Agape* Love is present, it will try to prevent the sin from going any further. For example, it would stop gossip before it begins. In other words, if we heard something negative about a brother or a sister, we would take it to the Lord first and ask Him what to do about it, *before* we would ever pass it on.

It's fascinating to me that non-believers know the authentic Christian when they see him. It proves that even though non-believers say they are not interested in Christian things, they are constantly searching for those genuine believers. Non-Christians seem to spot the *phonies* a mile away; whereas, we Christians are often fooled by our so-called "brothers and sisters." It's only God's authentic Love through us that will truly touch these unbelievers and bring them to Jesus. Our flowery and empty words *about* Jesus are not enough. Our actions must match our words in order for it to be true fruit bearing. In other words, we must be *living examples* of Jesus' Love!

1 John 3:10b asserts, "Whosoever doeth not righteousness is not of God, neither he that loveth *not* his brother." This means that if we are <u>not</u> truly loving others with God's Love, then we are showing the world that we're really <u>not</u> God's children at all. We might belong to Him, but we don't reflect Him in our lives.

The one who is actually abiding in Christ goes outside of himself to be Christ-like. He opens himself up, he stretches out his arms and *he loses himself in God.* The result is that *he finds himself in loving others*.

## Two Extreme Examples

I spoke with a young Christian man yesterday who has become very depressed and discouraged because of a debilitating illness. He said he no longer can see any purpose in living. He is so self-consumed at this moment that he cannot see that, yes, he is losing himself. But, not in God. He is losing himself *in his own problems.* And because of this, he has lost the will to live.

Now, I must be the first to admit that I have never been so ill that I've felt hopeless and purposeless. Therefore I confess that it's easy for me to *say* the things I am about to say because I've never truly experienced them for myself. And perhaps if I was in this young man's shoes, I would feel the same way he does. But *the Bible* says that no matter how sick we are, no matter what our circumstances are and no matter what others have done to us, the only way we can find ourselves is by loving others. The whole of God's Word is summed up in the first and second commandment–we are commanded to love (*agapao*) God and others. (Matthew 22:40) So, no matter where we are in life, God says *this is the answer*.

This young man *has* a family who loves him; he *has* parents who have given up everything for him; a wife who adores him; and children who look up to him. He has people all around him who love him and will do anything they can to make life easier for him. Isn't that enough to keep him hanging on? And, even if he doesn't "feel" like it, God has given him the authority and power to make *faith choices*–non-feeling choices to *overcome* his natural feelings in order to have the attitude that God desires. And I know God will be faithful to align his feelings to match those choices.

On the other hand, I have another dear friend, Cindy, who is in the same situation as the above gentleman. (We spoke of her earlier.) Only, Cindy continually makes faith choices to stand strong and let the Lord use her regardless of what is physically going on in her life. *She has lost herself in God.* She has been ill for almost five years. Last summer, the doctors told her the only chance of survival was a heart transplant. They were very nervous about the procedure because, with her diabetes, she was an extremely high-risk case. The chance of rejection was very high. She chose to risk it, however, and received a new heart last summer. Her prognosis is still uncertain, and in the meantime, she has suffered two other major illnesses. But, in spite of all this, Cindy has chosen to be a vessel of God's Love–not only to her husband and son, but to all of us who know her. We work with her every day and we are blessed by her unwavering commitment to the Lord. She has found herself in God and in loving others. What an example of Christ she is for all of us; always a smile, always a touch and always a concern for others! Truly, she <u>is</u> the queen of fruit bearers!

Scripture tells us that when we walk in *Agape* Love (the fruit of the Spirit), we glorify Him. God's Love and His glory can almost be seen as synonymous. 1 John 4: 8b says, "God is Love." Therefore when we show forth His Love, we reflect Him. And John 15:8 tells us that "Herein is my Father glorified, that ye bear much fruit." So, again, this kind of Love–this kind of fruit–is the sign of a true disciple. It's the chief mark of a Christian and the highest glory of God. (John 11:36))

## Jesus is the Fruit of Love

Christianity, then, is a religion of Love. If only we could love the way Jesus intends, everyone would see that it <u>is</u> the answer they are looking for. ***Jesus is that***

*Love*.  And He has called us to be His co-workers–His co-laborers and His partners–in spreading His gospel of Love to the world.  Our life is not just something to simply be enjoyed or derive happiness from, but an opportunity to pass along God's Love.

1 John 3:14 warns us, "He that loveth <u>not</u> his brother abideth in death."  This Scripture says that *if we are not loving, then we are dying*.  Wow!  And what's so tragic is that I see this very thing happening everywhere these days.  For example, the young man with the serious illness we just spoke about.  He's dying because he's separated from the true meaning of his life, which is *Love*.  In other words, God's Spirit in his heart is quenched and blocked because of his own doubt and unbelief.  Thus, God's Love is unable to penetrate his soul, let alone flow through him to others.  Abiding in God's Love not only means *receiving it from the Father*, but also *giving it to others*.

Abiding in Christ is what leads us to *walking like Him*. (1 John 2:6)  "The fruit of a life **in** Christ is a life **like** Christ," says Andrew Murray in his book, *Abiding in Christ*.  That power and that Love come only from abiding in Him.  Abiding lifts us above men's approval and gives us a teachable spirit. (1 John 3:18-19, 21-24) And those with a teachable spirit will continue to grow more and more into Christ's image.  Abiding, therefore, must always precede walking and glorifying Him.  If we abide, then, yes, we will bear much fruit. (John 15:5)

The apostle John notes in his thesis on abiding that the heaviest-laden branches seem to be the ones that always bear the most fruit. *As we esteem others better than ourselves; as we seek nothing for ourselves; as we live only for God; as we choose to be humble; as we take no offence; as we are always ready to serve; as we don't allow sin to have dominion over us; and as we are alive only to God and lose sight of ourselves, we will bear much fruit.*

The bottom line is that God calls us to give up our lives in order to win others to Christ. Are you willing to do this?

## Spiritual Warfare

A very important part of abiding in Christ is the ability to recognize the attacks of the enemy and to know what exactly to do about them. The Lord tells us in Psalm 91 that if we abide, *"He will keep us from the snare of the fowler* and *no evil will befall us*; He will deliver us and set us on high because we have known His Name."* He promises to keep us from harm because we have set our love *upon* Him and are abiding *in* Him. (Matthew 7:16; 1 John 1:5-6)

Knowing how to wage spiritual warfare will not only help us remain in the Holy Place, it will also enable us to continue to bring forth fruit in *all* circumstances. As we begin to abide on a daily basis, however, we'll find that we encounter the enemy more than ever before. **This occurs because we are beginning to reflect the Lord's image and the enemy is mad.** (That's one of the reasons for the warning at the beginning of this book.) We've become his "mark" and his "target." Consequently, part of our worship time in the Holy Place *must* be concerned with spiritual warfare. Luke 10:19 tells us: "Behold I give unto you power over all the power of the enemy and *nothing, by any means, shall hurt you.*"

Let me take you back to the temple for just a moment and show you some of the places the enemy loves to hide out. Maybe you have never seen this before.

## The Temple Walls

In preparation for our new DVD that is coming out this Fall, three of us at *King's High Way* (Debbie, Pastor Dave and I), have been studying the Inner Court wall of Solomon's Temple, the wall between the Inner Court and the Outer Court. I've never explored this area before, so what we are discovering is very exciting.

Before we begin, you might want to read these provocative Scriptures that refer to the "walls of our soul":

(Isaiah 60:18c) "Thou shalt call thy walls Salvation and thy gates Praise."

(Isaiah 26:1) "In that day, shall this song be sung in the land of Judah; We have a strong city; salvation will God appoint for walls and bulwarks."

(Isaiah 49:16) "Behold I have graven thee upon the palms of my hands; thy walls are continually before me."

(Isaiah 62:6a) " I have set watchmen upon thy walls."

(Jeremiah 1:18) "For, behold, I have made thee this day a defenced city, and an iron pillar, and brazen walls against the whole land." (See also Proverbs 25:28; Leviticus14:37-40; Ezekiel 27:11)

The Lord tells us in the above Isaiah 49:16 Scripture that our "walls" are continually before Him. If the walls of our soul are strong and there are no gaps, breaches or holes (meaning we have dealt with all the surface issues), then we'll be able to keep the enemy out by depending totally upon the Godly authority and power that the Lord has given us. However, if our walls have been broken down, are sagging or are "plastered over with untempered mortar" ("whitewashed walls" as Matthew 23:28 calls them), then we immediately become open to the enemy's arrows and our Godly strength will evaporate.[34]

---

[34]        Isaiah 30:12-13; Ezekiel 13:10-15; Nehemiah 4:10

See **CHART 10** ("Surface issues" in walls of our soul)

God wants us to see and acknowledge the sin and self that have accumulated in the walls of our soul.[35] He wants us to confess, repent and then give it all to Him, as we learned in Chapter Five. Afterwards, He wants us to rebuild the walls of our soul according to His instructions. He wants us to become "repairers of the breach" (Isaiah 58:12), "watchmen on the wall" (Isaiah 62:6) and "brazen walls" (Jeremiah 1:18). It's imperative to recognize the *surface issues* in the walls of our souls so that they don't become *root issues* or "strongholds" that attach themselves to the hidden chambers outside of our heart.

See **CHART 11** ("Root issues" in hidden chambers)

A stronghold is an issue that we haven't dealt with but simply buried in the hidden part of our soul. It's something we dwell upon, entertain over a period of time and eventually may even act upon. It's an area that our spirit does not have full control over and, thus, is wide open to attack from the enemy. We need to learn to identify these strongholds in our lives and then root them out, pull them down and destroy them. (Jeremiah 1:10)

---

[35]     James 4:7-9; Leviticus 14:33-48

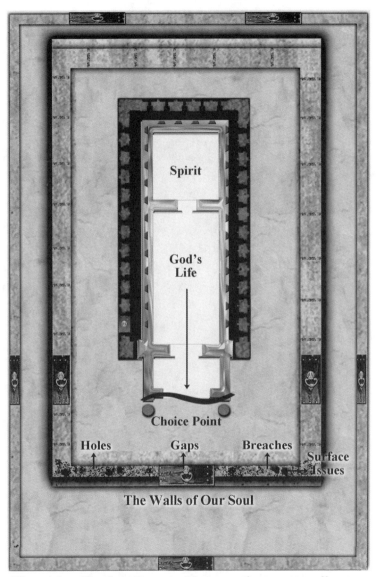

Chart 10    **Surface Issues**: Any negative or ungodly issue that tries to gain access to our soul.

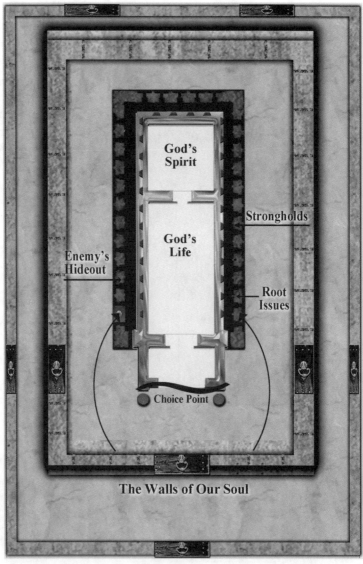

Chart 11   **Root Issues**: Any issue that has not been dealt
with and thus stored in the hidden chambers.

## Symptoms of a Stronghold

In Vito Rallo's outstanding book, *Pulling Down Strongholds*, he lists some symptoms of a stronghold. I thought it helpful to mention some of them here:

- Any persistent act of disobedience or sin habit that is uncontrollable
- Unrestrained behavior, i.e., language, anger or temper or violence
- Depression, mental breakdowns, confusion or fear
- Repeated failures, never able to fully succeed
- Poverty cycle, never able to have enough to live on
- Sickness and disease that "runs in the family" and that doesn't respond to prayer or medical treatment
- Uncontrolled desires: lust, perversion which results in sexual sins
- Addictions to drugs, alcohol, gambling, food, etc.
- Breakdown in family relations

Chapter Eight of Ezekiel talks about both surface and root issues and how, if not dealt with, they can become the enemy's hideout. In verse 12 it says, "Son of man, hast thou seen what the ancients of the house of Israel do in the dark, every man in the *chambers of his imagery*." If you look up the word "imagery" in *Strong's Exhaustive*

*Concordance of the Bible*, it says that it is "a figure carved in a wall." Remember in Chapter Four, we talked about Isaiah 64 and how "if we wait upon the Lord," *He will carve His image into the walls of our soul.* This, of course, is His will. However, in this passage here in Ezekiel, it tells us that unrighteousness is "carved into the walls" of the priests soul. Therefore, it opened them up to all sorts of enemy activity as you can see in the rest of the chapter.

Ecclesiastes 10:8 makes it even clearer: "He that breaketh an hedge, *a serpent shall bite him.*" In other words, if somehow our wall can be broken into and defiled, then we'll be totally vulnerable to the enemy's attacks. Nahum 3:17-19 confirms that demons encamp in the hedge. As long as we operate in the natural or soulish realm, we'll be vulnerable to the demonic attacks of the enemy. This is why the Lord warns us: "Do not give the devil a foothold." (Ephesians 4:27) Do not give him even a little opening or entrance.

## Cords of Sin

When talking about "strongholds,' Proverbs 5:22 is a very provocative Scripture. "His own iniquities shall take the wicked himself, and he shall be [held] with the *cords of his sins.*"

"Cords of sin" are spoken about in Isaiah 58:6-8 where they are called "bands of wickedness" or the cords that bind. Listen, "Is not this the fast that I have chosen? to loose the bands of wickedness, to undo the heavy burdens, and to let the oppressed go free, and that ye break every yoke... Then shall thy light break forth as the morning and thine health shall spring forth speedily: and thy righteousness shall go before thee; *and the glory of the Lord shall be thy rereward.*"

The Lord wants us to be "repairers of the breach," not only in our own temple, but also by "standing in the gap for others," praying for them and reaching out to them. He wants us to see that our own unconfessed sins, unresolved hurts and unvented negative thoughts (whatever has separated us from God) form chains or bands around us that will bind us. "Whatever is not of faith" or whatever we have not dealt with is what the enemy will use to keep us his captive and to "revenge God." (Romans 14:23c) Satan wants to defeat God's plans and purposes by using our own fleshly choices to kill, steal and destroy us. Consequently, it's not so much that our own natural thoughts, emotions, and desires are warring against us, but that the power of sin is using them for that very purpose.

Again, we must understand that once we are believers, neither Satan nor the power of sin has access to our new spirit, our new heart, or our new willpower. These areas are inviolate just as they were in Solomon's Temple. The analogy of the Temple's structure helps us to understand that a Christian *cannot* be "demon-possessed." Our spirit and heart cannot belong to God and to Satan at the same time. We will either have a *new heart* (Christ in us, our hope of glory), or an *old heart* (evil from birth and obviously, open to the enemy's attacks). *However, if we make fleshly choices that open up areas of our soul and our body to the enemy, we'll give him a "legal right" of involvement there.*

## Legal Rights

1 John 5:18-19 reads: "We know that whosoever is born of God sinneth not, but he that is begotten of God keepeth himself, and that wicked one toucheth him not." The word "toucheth" in the Greek is *haptomai*, which means "to fasten to, to cling to, to attach oneself to." Consequently, if we continue to make faith choices to confess, repent and follow God regardless of how we feel or what we think, the enemy cannot touch us. There will be no gaps, holes or breaches (no legal rights).

However, if we make fleshly choices to follow our sin or self over what God has shown us, we give the enemy an opening (a legal right) to fasten, cling and bind himself to us. We have given him the right to do so by yielding to the power of sin and creating a breach in our wall or hedge of protection. (Job 1:10; Isaiah 5:5-6; Ez.8:7-8)

As we learn to identify, acknowledge and give God not only the surface issues but also the root issues that He exposes, then the gaps, breaches and holes in the walls of our souls will begin to close up. We've all heard the term "standing in the gap." By going through the four steps of cleansing that we learned in Chapter Five, we will literally be standing in the gap, preventing the enemy from adding more "strongholds," more "anti-Christ carved figures" and more "mildew" to the walls of our soul.

Remember Isaiah 58:11-12: "And the Lord shall guide thee continually, and satisfy thy soul in drought, and make fat thy bones: and thou shalt be like *a watered garden*, and like *a spring of water*, whose waters fail not. And they that shall be of thee shall build the old waste places: thou shalt raise up the foundations of many generations; and thou shalt be called *the repairer of the breach*."

Speaking of being "repairers of the breach," check out Nehemiah 4:10-23. I find this passage fascinating. This is where Nehemiah is trying to re-build the Inner Court wall of the temple.

In verse 10 it says, "The strength of the bearers of burdens is decayed and *there is much rubbish so that we are not able to build the wall. And **our adversaries** said, They shall not know, neither see, till we come in the **midst among them** and slay them and **cause the work to cease**.*"

Nehemiah heard about their plan, so he set watchmen in "the lower parts behind the wall" and on the "higher places" with their swords, spears and bows in their hands. Once the enemy heard that the watchmen knew about them, it "brought their counsel to nought." From then on, half the wall builders worked and the other half held spears, shields and bows. "Every one had his sword girded by his side" and "none did put off their clothes [armor?]" until the wall was repaired.

What a great picture this gives us of exactly what our adversary is trying to do in us. It also shows us the importance of spiritual warfare and continually making the right choices to keep our walls strong.

### See **CHART 12**

As we become "repairers of the breach" in the wall and begin to build a firm foundation, Scripture assures us that we may be "those who are planted in the house of the Lord [who] shall flourish [which means blossom or bloom] in the courts of our God." (Psalm 92:13) In other words, as long as we abide in the sanctuary–in the presence of the Lord–we will bear fruit in our souls.

Something that thrills me as I grow older, is that the very next Scripture, verse 14, says, "they will still bring forth fruit in *old age*; they shall be fat and flourishing." I want to be that person! At least, the one that "brings forth fruit;" I'm not so sure about the "fat and flourishing" one!

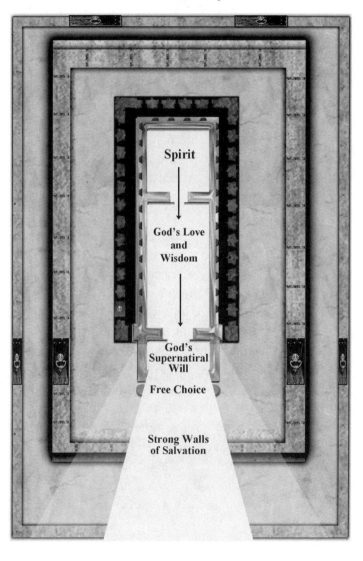

**Spirit**

**God's Love and Wisdom**

**God's Supernatiral Will**

**Free Choice**

**Strong Walls of Salvation**

Chart 12    **"Repairers of the Breach"**

# Spirit of Discouragement, Confusion and Depression

The picture of a broken-down wall around the temple, however, is very graphic and hits close to home because the spirit of confusion, discouragement and depression has become rampant among Christians these days. More than three quarters of the calls we get here at the ministry are from believers suffering from depression and discouragement. It's fascinating because back in the Old Testament book of Kings, the prophet Elijah, who brought the message of repentance to the nation of Israel, also struggled with discouragement and depression. If you recall, his archenemy was a controlling, manipulating and evil woman named Queen Jezebel. (See 1 Kings 18-19) Well, Revelation 2:20 tells us that in the *end times*, a period I believe is close, that same Spirit of Jezebel will come back to seduce Christians (especially leaders and those totally surrendered to the Lord) by robbing their hope in the Lord's faithfulness and undermining their confidence in Him. She wants to break down the walls of our soul in order to gain entrance. Her tactics are to fuel *discouragement, confusion and depression* in order to take control of our lives. She wants us to switch from the fruit of the spirit to the poison of self. And, she'll do whatever she can and use whatever hole she finds in order to do this.

The only way we can fight back is by making sure our Inner Court *wall* is strong. We must continually recognize the enemy's tactics to "divide and conquer." Then, in Christ's Name, learn to bind him and forbid him entrance.

## The Keys to the Kingdom

Speaking of binding the enemy, Matthew 16:19 teaches us that this principle holds the "keys of the kingdom." "I will give unto thee *the keys of the kingdom* of heaven: and whatsoever thou shalt bind on earth shall be bound in heaven: and whatsoever thou shalt loose on earth shall be loosed in heaven." (See also Matthew 18: 18)

The word "to bind" actually means to be put into bonds, to be tied up, to yoke, to harness or to join together. It can also mean to forbid, refuse, not allow, shut the door or bring into subjection. The word "to loose" in Matthew 18 means to break up, dissolve, unloose or melt away. It can also mean to permit, open or grant. *Binding and loosing are Hebrew idioms for exercising the Lord's power and authority*, and these, Jesus says, are the "keys" to the kingdom.

It's interesting because Adam Clark in his commentary on Matthew 16:19, says that when the Jews confirmed a man as a doctor of the law, they put into his hands the keys to the closet in the temple where the sacred books were kept, signifying that they were giving him the authority to teach what was to be permitted and what was to be forbidden.

These keys were a symbol of authority and the badge of the office. In like manner Jesus has given us that same authority and power *in His Name*. He has given us His authority "to bind" the enemy (to forbid him entrance) and His power "to loose" his strongholds (to break up and dissolve the ones already established). Because of Christ, we too, have the keys to the closet of the temple of our body. (1 Corinthians 3:16)

Again, picture the temple and its walls. If we know how to do spiritual warfare, when an arrow heads our way, we can, in Christ's Name, *forbid* its entrance. Likewise, when the Lord shows us our strongholds, we can, in Christ's Name, break them up and dissolve them. (Check out Psalm 89:40.)

## Binding and Loosing

We mentioned earlier that Jesus is always considered our example. What He did in many cases was simply *bind the enemy* (forbid him from speaking), rebuke him and then command him to flee. And, by doing so, He pulled down, broke up and dissolved many fortified hideouts and other walled defenses the enemy had erected.

We, also, by Christ's authority and power, can forbid and refuse to allow the enemy any more entrances into our souls, and we can, by Christ's authority, dissolve the strongholds already at root. As we mentioned, *undealt with* surface issues can become root issues in our hidden chambers. For example: feelings of resentment (one of those holes in the walls of our soul) can lead to the stronghold of bitterness (in the hidden chambers); confusion in our soul can lead to the stronghold of discouragement and depression; and feelings of betrayal can lead to distrust, etc. (Hebrews 12:15)

Another problem that often occurs when strongholds of bitterness, discouragement and betrayal are built, is that we then protect them by our <u>own</u> self-erected and walled defenses. However, because these are "<u>self</u>-erected" walls and not God-erected, they will <u>not</u> work. They not only won't hold back the enemy, they will actually allow him more territory to control. These, again, are the "untempered walls" and "white-washed walls" lightly covered with plaster, that Ezekiel 13:10 talks about. They are boundaries that *we* set up in the flesh which are nothing more than self-erected hedges that keep the enemy *in*, rather than *out*! Again Nahum 3:17 tells us that these defenses become hideouts and campgrounds for the enemy. ("snares of the devil," 2 Timothy 2:25-26, and "snares in our sides," Judges 2:2-3) The result is Nahum 3:19: *"There is no healing of thy bruise."* In other words, if we erect our own walls of protection and our own boundaries to cover our vulnerability, we won't be healed. Why? Because our foundation will still be cracked and our walls of salvation will still be weak and vulnerable. (Psalm 11:3) This is why the Lord wants all the strongholds loosed, broken up and dissolved.

When we ask the Lord to expose the hidden part of our soul and confess and repent of the things that He shows us, we will destroy, break apart and smash any deception around which the strongholds are built. In 2 Corinthians 10:4 we are told how to do this: "The weapons of our warfare are not carnal, but mighty through God to the pulling down of strongholds." (See also  Colossians 3: 5-11)  Thus, God is the One who exposes the breaches, cleans them out and then refills them with His Spirit. Our responsibility is to continually ask Him to do so. This cleansing doesn't happen automatically!

So, the only way we are ever going to be "conformed into His image" is by surrendering every emotion, every thought, every desire, every attitude, every fear and every breach and every stronghold–inside and out–that might create opportunities, entrances or holes for the enemy. There's a huge difference between simply defining the sin and actually pulling down the strongholds that helped produce it in the first place.

In 2 Corinthians 10:5-6 we are told our responsibility is to: "Cast down imaginations, and every high thing that exalteth itself against the knowledge of God, and [bring] into captivity every thought to the obedience of Christ;

And [have] in *a readiness to revenge all disobedience*, when your obedience is fulfilled." This, to me, is one of the lessons that God is trying to teach us. He wants to become our shield of protection and our brazen wall. (Isaiah 49:16) And the only way we can let Him do that, is by learning what the term "binding and loosing in Christ's Name" really means. We need to make the "walls of our soul" strong. As believers we have Christ's power and authority to either prohibit or to allow, to tear down or to build up, to cast down or to grant. Truly, the "keys" to the closet of our temple.

Other powerful Scriptures in regards to this area of binding and loosing are Matthew 12:27-30, Mark 3:27 and Luke 10:19. It's imperative that we learn to continually bind the enemy with chains (Psalm 149:8) and command him, in Jesus Christ's Name, to be gone.

Binding and loosing in His Name is part of abiding in the spirit. If we don't learn how to do this, it's analogous to taking off our grave clothes but not rolling away the stone.

Graham Powell notes in his book *Christian, Set Yourself Free* that "if as believers, we give ourselves to any sin, we give *legal ground* for demons to gain a measure of control in our lives. Conversely, when we obey God, a hedge of protection is built around our lives."

Now, we understand that demons *cannot* co-inhabit our spirit or our heart, but they *can* attach themselves to areas of our flesh that have <u>not</u> been submitted to the control of the Holy Spirit. Often these demons find a foothold in our lives even before we become believers. These creatures need to be exposed, confronted and expelled. In light of this, I truly believe a part of our conversion experience–our born again confession–should be the renouncing of any prior demonic activity and loosing any previous evil ties. Then, we could truly start off with a clean slate ("clean closets," you might say).

I have been in touch with several Christians recently who have struggled for years with demonic activity, yet were taught by their pastors that Christians cannot have demons. Thus, these precious people have suffered tremendous torment and have been the enemy's pawns. Once they began to understand the difference between their heart (which is Christ's) and their soul (which *can* be open to demonic activity if the walls of their salvation are not strong), and once they learned how to expose, cleanse and be delivered from, these entities, their lives have been fully restored. The only way they can now avoid these entities returning is by continuing to make faith choices that keep these beings on the outside of their hedge, or wall of protection. But again, if evil is already on the inside (and has already established strongholds because of previous demonic activity), it must be exposed and cast out.

# Bands of Love

God wants to control, lead and guide our lives through His reins of Love. Hosea 11:4 tells us that the Lord "drew them with cords of a man, with *bands of Love.*" What do reins or bands do? They control, lead and direct action. They guide and make a horse do what the rider wants. Without reins, the horse will go wherever he pleases.

The Lord continually tries to direct our lives through the leading of His Holy Spirit in us, His "reins of Love." If we thwart and quench His leading, then we give the enemy an opportunity to direct our lives through "chains of sin" (things of the flesh).

Psalm 32:9 and 8 seems to predict this constant choice of ours and instructs us, "Be not as the horse or as the mule, which have no understanding, whose mouth must be held in with bit and bridle." But let the Lord instruct you and teach you in the way you should go. Let Him guide you with His eye, which is the Spirit of the Lord in you.

Thus, you can see that the process of sanctification is <u>not</u> an instantaneous transition as some suppose, but often takes years before a person can truly come to the point of allowing Christ to be Lord in *every* area of his or her life.

Revelation 12:11 makes it very clear the way we overcome the enemy. It says the brethren overcame the enemy "by the blood of the Lamb, by the word of their testimony and by loving *not* their lives unto death." In other words, they were willing to continually surrender their lives to the Lord by dying to themselves. Romans 12:21 exhorts us, "Be not overcome of evil, but overcome evil with good." In other words, rather than let the enemy's "cords of sin" paralyze us, we must let God's "cords of Love" direct us. (Hosea 11:4)

## The Armor of God

*God* is the One who promises to protect us with His armor–the light of His countenance–but *we* are the ones who must be the "watchmen on the wall" continually choosing to put it on. Romans 13:12 tells us that we are to *cast off the works of darkness* and *put on the Armor of Light*.

It's very exciting because each piece of armor listed in Ephesians 6 seems to line up perfectly with our own internal architecture—spirit, heart, willpower, soul and body. Let's read Ephesians 6:13-19 all at once and see God's *Armor of Light* perhaps in a little different perspective.

See **CHART 13**

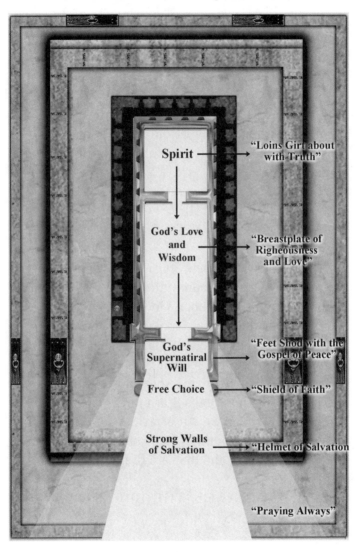

**Chart 13**     **Armour of God**
Ephesians 6:11-19

Ephesians 6:13: WHEREFORE TAKE UNTO YOU THE WHOLE ARMOR OF GOD, THAT YE MAY BE ABLE TO WITHSTAND IN THE EVIL DAY, AND HAVING DONE *ALL*, TO STAND.

This verse teaches us that the only way we can *stand* against the enemy of our souls is by having on the *whole* armor of God (the full Armor of Light with no dark part).

Verse 14: STAND THEREFORE, HAVING YOUR LOINS GIRT ABOUT WITH TRUTH

This speaks of the *new Spirit* (or new power source, life source or energy source) that we receive when we are born again. Remember, God's Holy Spirit and His Word working together are spoken of as the *truth*. Truth is what we must have securely "fastened" about our loins. *Loins* in Scripture are spoken of as the source of our procreation—the energizing source that brings *new life* into being. And it is God's Spirit through His Word that quickens new life in us. "It is *the Spirit that giveth life*; the flesh profiteth nothing. *The words that I speak unto you, they are spirit*, and they are life." (John 6:63)

AND HAVING ON THE BREASTPLATE OF RIGHTEOUSNESS,

In 1 Thessalonians 5:8, Paul amplifies the above verse by saying, "putting on the breastplate of faith and Love." This also symbolizes the *new Heart* that we receive as a result of our new birth–God's eternal Life in us, His supernatural Love and His Thoughts and His Power. (Romans 10:10)[32]

Verse 15: AND YOUR FEET SHOD WITH THE PREPARATION OF THE GOSPEL OF PEACE

The *new willpower* that God gives us at our new birth prepares and equips our souls (or our feet) with the gospel of peace. It's <u>His</u> Authority and <u>His</u> Power to *put off* the debris, dirt and filth in our own lives, and to *put on* Christ.

Using our supernatural willpower is what "shods" our feet (or our souls) for walking. Remember in John 13: 8-10 when Peter says to Jesus, "Thou shalt never wash my feet." Jesus answers him, "If I wash thee not, thou hast no part with me." Jesus is saying that unless we allow Him to daily *wash our feet* (our souls), we'll have no part of His Life.

Verse 16: *ABOVE ALL*, TAKE THE SHIELD OF FAITH, WHEREWITH YE SHALL BE ABLE TO QUENCH ALL THE FIERY DARTS OF THE WICKED

This verse speaks of our *free choice*. The choice to follow what God is prompting us to do; or the choice to go our own way. It's possible to possess God's supernatural Authority and Power and yet never choose to use it.  Again, to "be born in the Spirit," but never actually "walk in the Spirit."  This Scripture tells us that "above everything else," only our constant *faith choices* will shield, cover and protect us from the attacks of the enemy.

The only way we can protect ourselves from the enemy's arrows is by choosing to trust God, bind the enemy and loose his strongholds.  If we don't make these kind of *faith choices*, but simply go along with the tide of our emotions, our shield will be down and we'll open ourselves up for more of the devil's schemes.

### Verse 17: AND TAKE THE HELMET OF SALVATION

Salvation occurs in *our souls*.  Salvation means *to deliver, to bring into safety, to save or to heal*.  In the long-term spiritual sense, salvation means *freedom from the penalty of sin*, which is death.  In the short-term spiritual sense, salvation means *freedom from the power of sin* and the enemy that continually wants to control our lives.  As we put on that helmet of salvation over our "reined in" self-life, we'll not only be safe from the enemy's attacks, but also Christ's image will be carved into the walls of our soul.

### AND THE SWORD OF THE SPIRIT, WHICH IS THE WORD OF GOD

Up until this point, God has been talking about our *defensive armor*. Ephesians 6 now switches and refers to our *offensive armor*. Things we must do in order to stay free of the enemy and "walk in the Spirit." One thing that's imperative, is to always remember to carry *God's two-edged Sword* (His written Word in our hands). Jeremiah 51:20 talks about God and His Word being like our "battle ax."

Verse 18: PRAYING ALWAYS, WITH ALL PRAYER AND SUPPLICATION IN THE SPIRIT AND WATCHING THEREUNTO WITH ALL PERSEVERANCE AND SUPPLICATION FOR ALL THE SAINTS

Another offensive weapon we must use is *prayer*. We need to learn to pray in the power of the Spirit in order to rebuke, bind and command the enemy to leave, pleading the Blood of Christ over us. It's also critical that we constantly *pray* and beseech God on behalf of our brothers and sisters in the Lord. Prayer is our *defensive mechanism* and our *communication line to God*, not only for ourselves, but also for those we love and, yes, even for those who have despitefully used us.

And finally, verse 19: AND FOR ME, THAT UTTERANCE MAY BE GIVEN UNTO ME, THAT I MAY OPEN MY MOUTH BOLDLY, TO MAKE KNOWN THE MYSTERY OF THE GOSPEL.

This has always my prayer. That "the words of my mouth and the meditation of my heart would be acceptable" to Him. (Psalm 19:14)

Thus, learning how to abide in the Lord, guard against any outside influence and put on the Armor of God, is of the utmost importance.

## Warfare Prayer

In light of all that we have learned in this chapter, I've personally found it beneficial to pray a daily spiritual warfare prayer. Yes, the Holy Spirit must always be the One to lead, but often it's nice to have a guideline to follow, especially when we are first starting out. So, here's a sample of how you might want to pray. If this prayer doesn't suit your needs, then, by all means, let the Spirit lead and write a new one.

*Abba Father, King of the Universe, in the Name of Jesus, I ask you to search out and expose all my enemies and the tactics they employ against me. Open my eyes that I may see and understand the battle. Give me wisdom and understanding that I may lean on Your ways and not my own.*

*Reveal any root of bitterness, unforgiveness or iniquity that I may repent before you and take back any legal right given to the enemy. Bind the enemy that is*

*round about me and loose every stronghold that*
*established in my life. In the Name of Jesus and thru*
*His authority I say to my enemies, "the Lord rebuke you*
*for He is my defender and the lifter of my soul. I take*
*my stand against you, your temptations, deceptions and*
*snares in the Name of the Lord Jesus Christ."*

*Father, Creator of all things, let me not take my*
*stand alone, but fill me with Your Spirit. Empower me*
*to stand against the enemy and cover me with the blood*
*of Jesus. Release Your mighty angels to defend me. I*
*trust in You, Jehovah-Jireh, my provider, and I will not be*
*disappointed, for You are a shield about me. Amen.[11]*

---

This, then, is how we are to "abide in God's Spirit"–
remain in His presence–so that we *can* then bring forth
fruit that pleases Him.

Abiding in the Spirit is the culmination of being born
anew by His Spirit, being cleansed by His Spirit and
worshiping in the Spirit. The next step is to actually *walk*
*in the Spirit*, which will glorify Him.

# Chapter Seven Questions

1) What does it mean to "abide in the Spirit" or "abide in the Lord"? (Psalm 91:9, 14)

2) Can you explain the subtle differences between abiding in the Spirit and walking in the Spirit?

3) Explain the parallel between the secular business of growing grape vines and producing fruit and Christians who are in the sanctification process.

4) What is the greatest fruit that we can produce as believers? (John 13:35; 1 Corinthians 13:2, 13)

5) What must we do in order to be the Lord's "friends"? (John 15:14; Proverbs 22:11)

6) What gives phony Christians away? What is it that non-believers see in them? (1 John 3:10b)

7) A part of abiding in Christ is the ability to recognize the attacks of the enemy and knowing what to do about them. Why is it that the more mature we get in the Lord, the more attacks we seem to receive?

8) What are some of the things *we* should do to protect ourselves from the enemy's attacks? (Luke 10:19; Romans 13:12)

9) What is a "stronghold"? What must we learn to do with them? (Jeremiah 1:10; James 4:7-11)

10) There are three prevalent areas that the enemy seems to attack in Christians. What are they and why does the enemy choose these? (Revelation 2:20)

11) Matthew 16:19 speaks about the "keys" to the Kingdom. What are they and what do they do?

12) Why is it so important to put on the Armor of God everyday? (Ephesians 6:13-20)

# Warfare Prayer

Dearest Lord: I desire to be a reflection of Your image so that my family, friends and others will see You in me and want what I have. Therefore, I choose to give You anything in me that would prevent my hearing directly from Your Spirit. I present my body as a living sacrifice, holy, acceptable unto You, which is my reasonable service. And I choose *not* to be conformed to this world but to be transformed (into Your image) by the renewing of my mind that I may prove what is Your good, acceptable and perfect will. (Romans 12:1-2)

I choose to "put on" the whole armor of God that I might be able to stand against the wiles of the enemy, having done all to stand strong. First of all, I choose to stand by having my loins girt about with truth and having on the breastplate of righteousness and Love guarding my heart. Next, I choose to shod my feet with the preparation of the Gospel of peace. Above all, I take up the shield of faith by which I can quench all the fiery darts of the enemy. Finally, I put on the helmet of salvation and the sword of the Spirit, which is the Word of God. (Ephesians 6:13-17) Praying always and on every occasion in the power of the Holy Spirit, keeping alert and persistent in praying for Christians everywhere.

*And that utterance may be given unto me, so I may open my mouth boldly to make known the mystery of the gospel, for which I am an ambassador in bonds; and that I may speak boldly, as I ought to speak.* (Ephesians 6:13-19)

And above all, I choose to put on *AGAPE*, which is the bond of completion. (Colossians 3:14)

# Chapter Eight
## How to *Walk in the Spirit*, Reflecting Him

## Controlled by the Spirit

So we see that abiding in the Lord and spiritual warfare must go hand in hand. Abiding in His presence involves companionship, communion, fellowship, mutual delight and decision making; whereas, spiritual warfare involves being a watchman on the wall protecting this relationship and always keeping an eye on the health of our soul. These are the things that build a firm foundation of faith so we are able to then "walk in the Spirit," sharing His heart with others. Walking with the Lord allows His image to penetrate our souls.

Abel, Enoch, Noah and Abraham all "walked with the Lord." (Genesis 5:22; 6:9) Each humbly sought His presence, watched over their own souls and the Lord rewarded them by revealing His glory. Interestingly, Scripture does not tell us exactly what Enoch did. I doubt it was anything spectacular or noteworthy. Yet, the Word tells us that "he walked with God." He was obviously someone very special to the Lord. Likewise, Noah found grace in the eyes of the Lord and thus the Lord shared His heart with Him. And, of course, as we said Scripture records Abraham as the Lord's "friend."

(James 2:23; Isaiah 41:8)  David Wilkerson comments, "to have the Creator of the Universe call you His friend seems almost beyond human comprehension."

Daily abiding in the Lord and doing warfare is the only way that a firm foundation for walking with the Lord can be built.  Bob Sorge says, "We must develop a secret history with God *before* He gives us a public one."

## The Glory of God

Scripture promises those who "walk in the Spirit" will attain the Kingdom of God.  However, as shared before, the way to this glory is often through suffering. The greater the suffering, the greater the glory.  In other words, the more we resemble Christ in spirit, power and action through suffering, the more we will glorify Him. Therefore, true sons and daughters of God will probably endure more trials than those of the world.  Read that again!  Because so often we hear preachers say just the opposite.  Scripture, however, tells us that "we must through much tribulation enter into the kingdom of God." (Acts 14:22)

Again, Christ is our example.  He was despised and rejected.  Isaiah tells us that "He was wounded...oppress ed...afflicted... Yet, it pleased the Lord to bruise Him and put Him to grief." (Isaiah 53: 5,7,10)  The way to future glory for us is through a similar path.  We are called to be "like Christ."  Suffering was a part of His life and it will be a part of ours also. God has designed it that way. Suffering is what leads to more glory for Him...less of us and more of Him.

Throughout Scripture we see God's pattern of abasement and then exultation. John 12:24 lays it out plainly. "Verily, verily, I say unto you, Except a corn of wheat fall into the ground and die, it abideth alone: but if it die, it bringeth forth much fruit."

Remember the story of Moses in Exodus 34. After fleeing Egypt, he was certainly brought and humbled. But, if you recall, after his encounter with the Lord on Mount Sinai, he was so radically changed that his face shone with the glory of God. *Glory is the result of being emptied of self and then filled with Christ and His presence.* A person's countenance is simply the outward expression of what is in his heart. Moses *externally* reflected the glory of God that he was experiencing *internally*. And the same experience can also be true of us. Psalm 34:15 validates this, "Those who look to Him for help will be lightened." In the Hebrew, the word is *sparkle* or *radiant*!

I recently received a beautiful letter from a prisoner who expresses this same thing only in a little different way. Listen:

"I find myself with a moment of unobstructed clarity of thought which is allowing me to faintly grasp the outer edges of the unspeakable joy that awaits our longing hearts when we see the Lord. Oh to see and touch our master's face. Will His face be familiar? Will it be like looking upon a long ago departed loved one's face? Will the radiance of His glory spill over us as a warm liquid love? Will His voice wash over us as waves of immeasurable, soothing sensation? Oh, to see His face! What glory awaits us!"

Paul talks about this glory in Galatians 1:15-16 when he says that God called him from birth to "reveal His Son." What Paul is saying here is that when Jesus becomes our life itself, others will see His reflection in us just as they did with Moses. Moses spent 40 days and nights in communion with the Lord and as a result his face shone with the glory of God. When we become one with the Lord through cleansing, worship and abiding, we too, will be able to reflect His image. When we live our lives with the purpose of glorifying Him, the invisible God becomes visible in us for all to see.[36]

See: Psalm 96:2;.43:5; 29:2; 90:17.

## An Example: Refiner's Fire

Recently, some women I know were having a Bible study and they came across Malachi 3:3: "He will sit as a refiner and purifier of silver." This verse puzzled them as to what it really meant about the character and nature of God. One of the women offered to find out about the process of refining silver and get back to the group

---

[36]     2 Corinthians 3:2-3; 11:30; Psalm 96:7-8; 115:1;
        John 7:18; 17:4; Romans 8:17; Isaiah 24:15

at their next Bible Study. That week the woman called a silversmith and made an appointment to watch him at work. She didn't mention anything about the reason for her interest beyond her curiosity about the process of refining silver. As she watched the silversmith, he held a piece of silver over the fire and let it heat up. He explained that in refining silver, *one needed to hold the silver in the middle of the fire where the flames were hottest so as to burn away all the impurities.* The woman thought about God holding us in such a hot spot. She went over and asked the silversmith if it was true that he had to remain in front of the fire the whole time the silver was being refined. The man answered that *he not only had to sit there holding the silver, but he had to keep his eyes on the silver the entire time it was in the fire.* He said that if the silver was left a moment too long in the flames, it would be destroyed.

The woman was silent for a moment. Then she asked the silversmith, "How do you know when the silver is fully refined?"

He smiled at her and answered, *"Oh, that's easy. It's done **when I see my own image in it!**"*[37]

Remember this story, if today, you are feeling the heat of that fire. God has His eye on you and will keep watching you until He sees His own image in you–until

---

[37]     Sent to me by David Lujan, Avenal Prison

He carves it into the "walls of your soul." Isaiah 24: 15 tells us that we must continue to glorify the Lord in midst of the fire.

Jesus is the full revelation of God's glory and if He abides in us and we in Him, His glory will shine forth in our lives. We are His arms and legs. Now, others might not see our face shining as they did Moses', but they *will* see His Love, wisdom and power coming forth from our lives.

It's interesting because the very first time Moses saw God's glory was the first time he ever worshiped Him. (Exodus 34:6-8) Again, there seems to be a connection between worship and the revelation of God's glory. Worshiping God not only changes us, it also allows us to reflect and mirror more and more of His image.

## Mirror Images

To mirror something means to perfectly reflect a person or a thing; to declare it; to manifest it and to exhibit its behavior or characteristics. It means to express its features or set forth the same image.

How often we say, "I see Jesus in you. I see Him in your eyes. I see Him in the kind and thoughtful things you do." What we really are saying is that by doing Godly actions that person is reflecting God's character. (Isaiah 42:12, Psalms 45:17)

David Wilkerson, again in one of his recent Newsletters, comments that "God's glory is a revelation of His nature and attributes."[38] By doing Godly actions, a Christian is simply showing forth the Lord's attributes– His Love, compassion, mercy, etc. Therefore, reflecting Him *properly* is of the utmost importance to the Lord. For example, Moses in Numbers 20:7-12 misrepresented the Lord's character when he *struck the rock* for water rather than simply *speaking to the rock* as the Lord had instructed. Moses, here, represented a vengeful God rather than a merciful God, who is always loving and ready to forgive. Matthew 5:44 tells us "Love your enemies, bless them that curse you, do good to them that hate you and pray for them which despitefully use you." This is what the Lord would do. This is His character.

Thus, Moses misrepresented God's character and the Lord punished him harshly by not letting him enter the promised land. **The Lord made a big issue here that representing Him properly is of the utmost importance**. Three times God mentions this incident in Scripture. Three times the Lord reproves Moses for not sanctifying Him in the eyes of Israel. (Numbers 20:12; 27:14; Deuteronomy 32:51)

Without question, how we represent the Lord with others is critical.

---

[38]     *Times Square Church Pulpit Series*, "The Effects of Seeing The Glory of God."

How do you reflect Him with your spouse?   With your children?  With your friends?  Co-workers?  Family? Are you the first to get angry and condemn them, like Moses did with the rock?  Or, do you show them God's compassion and gentleness?  Remember, the Lord wasn't a softy; He wasn't a pushover.  When needed, He knew just how to take a strong stand in Love.  He knew that perfect balance between longsuffering Love and tough Love, between grace and righteousness and between mercy and judgment. (1 Timothy 1:5)

But, when we <u>do</u> correctly show forth the Lord's nature, He is glorified in us.[39]  We are to be mirrors of His presence in us.[40]  If we do this, Psalm 30:12 tells us that our glory will sing praise to Him.  And Christ–not we–will be lifted up.

Christ Jesus was a living illustration of the invisible God.  By constantly glorifying the Father, He honored Him and gave the world reason to love and obey Him themselves.  We are to do the same.  We are to embody the actual Life of Jesus in our lives.  *The Gospel can never be understood by precept alone.  It must have a corresponding example*!  Our lives need to be a living illustration of it.  No other illustration is as effectual as the souls and the spirits of "spiritual" Christians. *It is impossible that the gospel should take effect or be understood without illustration.*  If our witness as

---

[39]     Philippians 3:3; John 15:8; Psalms 89:15; 98:3
[40]     Exodus 15:2, Psalms 84:5

Christians contradicts what the gospel says, our testimony will be destroyed.[41] And we have seen this tragically happen over and over again.

## The Chief Objective of Man

The Westminster Catechism tells us that the chief and highest end of man is to glorify God. David Wilkerson says, "We are to mirror His Love to the world through our own lives of sacrifice and devotion."[42]

Paul confirms this, "But we all, with open face beholding as in a glass the glory of the Lord, are changed into the same image from glory to glory, even as by the Spirit of God." (2 Corinthians 3:18)

*Cleansing, worshiping and abiding are the means by which we are changed more and more into His image, but glorifying Him–reflecting that image to others– is what will bring them to Christ.* Cleansing, worshiping and abiding are things we do on the *inside*, whereas glorifying God is something that happens on the *outside*. 1 Corinthians 11:7 validates that man is "the glory and image of God." We were created not only for fellowship, but also to be conformed into His image so that that image can be portrayed through us to others.[43] That's our destiny and our highest purpose as Christians. We are to be the express image of Christ and His person, just as He was the "express image of His Father." (Hebrews

---

41      Material from a lecture called "Glorifying God"
        by Rev. Charles G. Finney, March 27, 1839.
42      From *World Challenge Pulpit Series*, David Wilkerson, November 05
43      Psalms 29:2; 96:6-9; 1 Corinthians10:31

1:3) It's the whole reason Jesus came and the reason He died–to restore man to his original purpose and calling. "Not unto us, O Lord, not unto us, *but unto Thy Name give glory...*" (Psalm 115:1)

Thus, we must allow Him to remove every hindrance in our lives that prevents His image from shining through us and revealing His full worth. Then <u>He</u> can be seen and acknowledged by all. He is glorified when <u>His</u> holiness, <u>His</u> Love and <u>His</u> righteousness can be seen in us. God's glory simply means His manifested holiness.[44]

Glorifying God is something we do in public. It's the outward manifestation of His Life in us. Cleansing, worshiping and abiding are where the transformation occurs, but reflecting His image is the result. In other words, after worship comes glory. (2 Chronicles 5:13)

## I See My God in You

Cindy Blackamore wrote a beautiful poem about seeing God's glory in others. Listen:

> "The God we serve is invisible;
> we know that this is true
> But friend, I tell you of a truth
> That I see God in you.

---

[44]     Exodus 15:11; Isaiah 6:3

Though God may be invisible unto my naked eye
I see His hand is working
And this fact I can't deny.

The Love that's written on your heart,
The smile on your face
The little things you do for me
The warmth of your embrace.

The kind words you have spoken,
The earnest of your prayer
Your willingness to serve me
The evidence you care.

The wisdom you have shown me
I know He's given you
For when I've looked into His Word
I found your words were true.

So yes, our God is invisible, but Him I plainly see
For when I look into your eyes
I see my God in thee!"

Sounds like Philippians 1:20 which says "that with all boldness...Christ shall be magnified in my body."

## The Link to Revival

Demonstrating God's glory in our lives is the key to revival. No words need to be shared. All that's needed to convey the message is our life.

Being a true reflection of Christ is as important today as it was in the Old Testament. As we mentioned earlier, from Israel's point of view the temple's true purpose was to be a light and inspiration for all humanity, pointing the way to the Lord. Remember, it was the place where God met with His creation, the place that God dwelt or inhabited. The temple was built to manifest God's glory. It sat on Mt. Moriah where His glory could be seen for miles around. It was a reflection of who God was and the soul and conscience for the whole world. (Exodus 25: 8; 15:2) Remember, the windows of Solomon's Temple were narrow on the inside and wide on the outside in order to capture the Light from God's presence and emanate it outward. These were called "closed windows" and they adorned the Holy Place and the Vestibule.[45] Again, can't you just imagine what a sight it must have been looking up at the temple from the rest of Jerusalem? Scripture says, "a city that is set on a hill cannot be hidden" (Matthew 5: 14); and this certainly must have described Jerusalem at that time. 2 Chronicles 7:3 tells us that "when the children of Israel saw the glory of the Lord upon the house, they bowed themselves with their faces to the ground and worshiped the Lord."

Now, it doesn't matter if that glory comes directly from the Shekinah Glory in Solomon's Temple or through the Spirit of God in a believer, it simply reveals that the Lord is present. How desperately our families, our friends and our children need to see this kind of manifestation. I really believe if this occurred on a large scale, it would

---

[45]     From *Secrets of the Temple* by Rabbi Moshe Chaim Luzzatto.

revolutionize the church.  God wants us to be mirrors of *His* Spirit in our hearts, revealing the light of *His* presence, *His* character and *His* nature in every-thing we do.

## Glorifying Him in *ALL* Things

It is, therefore, essential that we try to reflect Him in all things.  His glory is the intrinsic excellence of His nature and His moral attributes.  His declarative glory means His renown, His reputation and the estimation in which He is held.  By exhibiting *His* spirit, temper and character, we declare His glory, just as Jesus did.  As a man, Jesus was engaged in glorifying His Father in everything.  Thus, He gave the world occasion to admire, love and obey the Father.  We are to illustrate that very same spirit.

Matthew 5:16 exhorts us to, "Let your light so shine before men, that they may see your good works, and glorify your Father which is in heaven."

We are to represent the Lord in our homes and with our families.  In our businesses we must manifest God's character.  In our recreation, we should reflect His image. In the choice of our entertainment and the books we read, we need to have a Godly balance.  In our houses and furnishings, we are to represent the Lord.  And, the same thing should be evident in what we eat and the health of our bodies. If we don't do these things, we are not only misrepresenting Him, we are actually dishonoring Him, the exact opposite of glorifying Him.

## A Few Examples: When You Think They are not Looking

Speaking about misrepresenting the Lord, we recently witnessed a pastor in a restaurant using foul language because his food wasn't served on time. The poor waitress was humiliated and everyone around him was absolutely shocked. What did that misrepresentation of Christ do to that waitress?

Who knows where she was spiritually. Maybe she was really close to attending some church or going to some Bible Study or making some inner commitment to God. After hearing that outburst from a known pastor, what did she think? One only can imagine!

In a similar incident, a young boy recently told me about an elder in his church who came into the video store where he worked and picked up several X-rated (not R-rated, but X-rated) movies. The boy said they weren't rated X for violence, but nudity. What did this incident say to this young boy? Matthew 23:3 tells us that there are those who *say* "don't do this" and "don't do that", but they themselves do those things! What kind of a "living example" are we when we do these things? Rather than bring others to Christ, we push them away.

And finally, Chuck and I visited a church recently where we were *not* known. We sat down for a few minutes and watched some of the churchgoers. Their sad, long, joyless faces were startling. All of us have bad days occasionally–days where we don't feel well–but this was different. Most of the people we saw had joyless, empty, lifeless faces that would be enough to turn any non-believer away. Non-believers need to see something in us that will make them want what we have. (They need to see that we have been with Jesus.) This church group certainly didn't possess it.

Unfortunately, non-believers form their opinions of the Lord by the lives and the tempers of the Christians they see and know. Therefore, in a broad sense, their opinions of Christ and their eternal futures really depend upon our own lives and how we represent Christ.[46] Only when we put Him on display with our words *and our deeds*, is He then glorified. Thus, the more we become like Him, the more He will be glorified.

How often we hear other Christians say, "I want to glorify God." What exactly do they mean by that? They probably just mean they want to do what Christ would want. Well again, let's use Jesus as our example. How did He glorify God? He glorified God *by accomplishing the work that the Father had sent Him to do*. Listen to John 17:4: "I have glorified Thee on the earth: I have

---

[46]      Again, some of this material taken from "Glorifying God" article by Rev. Charles G. Finney, 1839.

finished the work which Thou hast given Me to do." The work that Jesus was sent to do can be summed up in three words: a life of *service, sacrifice and suffering*.

And, it's the same with us. Once the process of transformation has been established, then, the work the Lord has for *us* is the same as it was for Christ–a life of sacrifice, service and suffering.

So far in this book, we have talked a great deal about sacrifice and about suffering, but we've not yet explored the subject of serving others, which is a major part of walking by the Spirit.

## Serving Others

If you recall, in the Gospel of Matthew Jesus tells us that He did not come to *be* served, but *to* serve. Jesus' life was a life of serving. He constantly humbled Himself and gave of Himself. And He tells us in Scripture to do the same: "whosoever will be great among you, let him be your minister." (Matthew 20:26-28) Just as Christ on the Cross gave Himself for all of us, He wants us to give ourselves to others by loving them and putting their will and desires above our own. If we truly want to glorify God, then we must always have a servant's attitude. *We do not exist just for ourselves, but to fulfill the work God has given us to do and that involves the giving of ourselves for others.*

As Christians, we will be constantly asked to give up (or sacrifice) our own desires, goals and dreams–to die to ourselves in order to live for others. As we said previously, this kind of life often includes suffering just as it did for Jesus.[47]  But, what's amazing is that the higher we rise in being like Christ, the more we'll *want* to serve others. This was Jesus' heart and the more we are conformed to His image, the more it will become our heart also. The way we serve others best is by truly loving them–by totally giving ourselves over to the Lord so that His Love can be manifested through us.

Ask yourself this question: If I see someone in need, what is my heart's response? Do I pass them by without so much as a care? Or do I stop to help them no matter what the cost to me? This reflects your "heart condition." A servant is one who is always ready to help his brother in need, refresh the Body and edify others. See Proverbs 17:17.

Again, Jesus is our example. His heart was always ready to serve, to sacrifice and even to suffer if He had to. He died not only for our redemption, but also to show us *how to live, how to love* and *how to serve*. God's glory was manifested in Jesus perfectly. Remember, His Life was an exact pattern of what the Father desires ours to be like: the brightness of His glory. Oneness with Him is the only thing that allows His *Agape* Love to flow through us to others. (John 17:11, 21-23) Jesus knew that He could only love *as the Father gave Him the ability*. The

---

47        Some material taken from Pastor Chuck Long's article "Glorifying God." See www.faithbibleohio.com

choice to be a cleansed vessel was His responsibility, but the actual work itself was always done by the Holy Spirit. And it's the very same with us. It's the Spirit's Love, power and ability; we are just the willing instrument that He uses.

Jesus could do nothing but what He saw the Father do. He modeled "dependent obedience" for us. He relied upon the Father for everything just as we are to do upon Christ. (1 John 1:2) Jesus' life was the fulfillment of what was written about Him in the Word. Jesus was the "*living Word.*" And we need to be living examples, exact representations and true demonstrations of Christ so that others might truly want what we have.

## Our Purpose As Christians

In order to make Christ-likeness a reality in our lives, we need the power of His resurrection. Christ humbled Himself (i.e., chose to set Himself aside) and was able to do the work of a servant, only because He depended upon the Spirit to do the work. As a result, the glory of God was shown in everything He did. In like manner, only the inflowing of Christ's Life from our hearts out into our lives, makes it possible for us to reflect the Lord in all we do. Jesus said, "*I am the Vine. You are the branches.*" (John 15:5) Just so, Christ's Life must flow through us in order to reach others. <u>He</u> is the Vine and <u>we</u> are the branches. However, His Life can only flow through us if we are cleansed, worshiping and abiding in Him. (Psalm 92:2)

See **CHART 14**

Note: I've turned the temple upside down to make it easier to see and also to emphasize the process of sanctification—the five steps—needed to reflect His Life: *Following His Spirit*; *being cleansed by His Spirit*; *worshiping in His Spirit*; *abiding in His Spirit* and, then, *walking by His Spirit*.

If we are doing these things, then we'll be able to walk as He walked (John 15:10); think as He thought; speak as He spoke; and act as He did because *He is the One* doing these things. He is just doing them through us.

Jesus was *in* the world and yet, the Word tells us, He was <u>not</u> of it. We must do the same. We are to live in the world and yet show by our godly lives that we are not of it. This is our mission and our goal—to make Him known to the world by showing forth His Love, His ways and His power. Again, David Wilkerson says, "We fulfill our life's purpose only as we begin to love others as Christ loved us."[48] We do this not just by words (as we have seen, this often leads to hypocrisy), but by our entire person—through our actions, our disposition and our conduct. We must so represent the Lord that others, just by seeing us, will know what He is like.

"Let your light so shine before men, that they may see your good works, and glorify your Father which is in heaven." (Matthew 5:16)

---

[48]          *World Challenge Pulpit Series*, David Wilkerson, April 2005

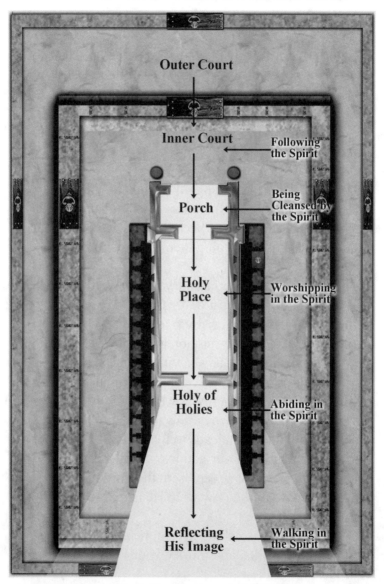

**Chart 14      Our Purpose as Christians**

# An Illustration

Think of this interesting analogy: Compare the *sun* illuminating the heavens and earth to a *lamp* lighting the inside of your home. The lamp lighting your home, does in its own little way, what the sun accomplishes for the whole earth. In like manner, each of us *in our own small sphere* can do what God in Christ did for the entire world.

Read Luke 11:33-35 again in this context: "No man, when he hath lighted a candle, putteth it in a secret place, neither under a bushel, but on a candlestick, that they which come in may see the light. The light of the body is the eye [the mind]: therefore, when thine eye is single [minded], thy whole body also is full of light; but when thine eye is evil [corrupted], thy body also is full of darkness. Take heed, therefore, that the light which is in thee be not darkness [quenched]. If thy whole body, therefore, be full of light, having no part dark, the whole shall be full of light, as when the bright shining of a candle doth give thee light."

Remember **CHART 7,** page 104. This is that "spiritual Christian" raising up Christ's Life, not his own.

Unfortunately, as we have shared, much of the Christian Body these days are like lights that are "hidden under a bushel." See **CHART 8,** page 106.

These are "carnal Christians" who have Christ's Life hidden under their own. Their lives reflect something completely different than what the Scriptures teach us about Christ and a relationship with Him. This, to me, is why the Christian body is in such turmoil and why there are so many divorces, broken homes and relationships. Consequently, it's imperative for us to *recognize our own need for change, cleansing, worship* and *abiding.* It's imperative in these last days that we become a fountain of His genuine Love and Life, <u>not</u> seeking blessings for ourselves, but only for the glory of God. Our future and the future of our children depend upon it.

2 Chronicles 5:11-14 tells us that it was only <u>after</u> the priests came out of the Holy Place, full of the Spirit of the Lord that the glory of the Lord filled the temple. In like manner, Scripture tells us that when we come forth from "abiding with the Lord," we too, will be full of the Spirit and God's glory. Christ's light will then shine forth from us and His glory will become our defense, our covering, our canopy and our protection. Isaiah 4:5-6 confirms this, "the Lord will create upon every dwelling place of Mount Zion, and upon her assemblies, a cloud and smoke by day, and the shining of a flaming fire by night: for *upon all the glory shall be a defense.*" This is saying that not only will we be filled with His Spirit, but that His Spirit will be our protection. His glory will shelter us, protect us and shield us from the intense struggle predicted to come upon the earth. In other words, once again, God will put His pillar of cloud and fire around His Church for comfort and for direction.

These manifestations and blessings will come only *after* we have learned to walk by His Spirit and glorify Him. Remember Psalm 92, which told us that those who are transplanted in the House of the Lord shall blossom in His Courts with the beauty of the Lord. That beauty is the "beauty of <u>His</u> holiness". Again, the parallel is here.

## Blessings that Result From Glorifying Him

After the priests worshiped the Lord, they came out from the Holy Place, stood on the steps and began to bless the people. A blessing means a bestowal of good. (Genesis 12:2; Isaiah 19:24; Zechariah 8:13; Proverbs 10:22) It means receiving a gift. In the Old Testament, receiving the father's blessing was paramount for direction in one's life. Now, we don't observe this custom in our families anymore, but how many of our children would give anything to hear their father's verbal blessing upon their lives.

In the New Testament, blessing (*eulogia*) means to speak well of someone, to consecrate them or to acknowledging God's goodness in their lives. (Luke 2:28; 6:28; 24:51; James 3:9a) In light of this, I have lately been asking the Lord to "bless" my children's lives. Obviously, I have always prayed and sought God's will in their lives, but lately I have been <u>specifically praying God's blessings (or favor) over my children's lives</u>. And, it seems to have made a huge and visible difference.

Blessings can come in a variety of ways. But there are two specific ways of blessing that are important and fit perfectly into the picture we are trying to paint.

1) As mentioned above, blessings can come as an act of bestowing a favor. This was often called an "inherited blessing." Again, we see this in the Old Testament, as sons would seek a blessing from their fathers as an official last will and testament. (Genesis 48:15-22) This is also the type of blessing or benediction that was given to the people in the temple court after the worship service.

2) There is another kind of blessing, however, called an "evaluative blessing" (*maharismos*) which means that those who live according to God's instructions will experience fulfillment and well-being. Scripture tells us that people who endure trials and yet, still choose to live according to God's Word, will be blessed.[49]   Peter even talks about a "spirit of glory" that will rest upon us. Also, anyone who perseveres in obedience in the face of persecutions will be rewarded. Clearly, blessings come not only from hearing God's Word, but also from doing what His Word says. (Revelation 1:3;14:13)

## The Name of the Lord

Numbers 6:23-27 is a very interesting passage in connection with receiving this last type of blessing. These Scriptures tell us that **the *Name* of Christ must always <u>precede</u> the blessing**. Listen: "They shall put

---

[49]     James 1:12; 5:11; 1 Peter 3:14; 4:14

*My Name* upon the children of Israel and [then] I will bless them." This means that those who reveal Christ's Name are assured of fulfillment, well-being and purpose in the Lord.

Now, *name* in the broad sense means authority, character, title, dignity, rank, majesty, power, excellence. Our *name* is who we are and who we are identified with. A name is connected with sight and perception. Remember Solomon's Temple was seen as a place where God's Name resided: "I will put My Name there forever." (1 Kings 9:3) In 1 Kings 8, this is referred to six separate times. (Verses 17, 19, 20, 43, 45, and 48)

Our "name" is what distinguishes us from others. New names were bestowed upon men in the Bible to show that something new had entered their life. Abram's name was changed to Abraham, signifying the beginning of a new man. Sarai was changed to Sara because she was endowed with new powers. And, Saul became Paul. (Acts 13:9) A new name meant a new chapter was happening.

Therefore, when Scripture speaks of being "in His Name," it means being in His likeness, in His Person and in His character. It's a way of stating that God dwells here. **It's a demonstration of His presence, in which we manifest His divine Name**, His character, His likeness and image. 2 Thessalonians 1:12 tells us that "the Name of our Lord Jesus Christ may be glorified in [us], and [we] in Him."

# Ask in My Name

Thus, we see that manifesting Christ's Name must be evident in our lives *before* a blessing can be received. Here's my point: Throughout the Gospel of John, He tells us to "ask in My Name." We have all read this Scripture a hundred times and thus, in obedience, we have simply attached "in His Name" to all our prayers. Well, I believe there's a much deeper meaning here than just "asking in His Name." **We must literally *be* in His Name. Not just born anew by His Spirit, but actually walking by His Spirit, reflecting His image, His character and His Name**. In other words, we are to pray our prayers and our petitions when we are truly glorifying Him. And if we do so, *then* we will receive His blessings and our prayers will be heard. Consequently, the reason our prayers are so often <u>not</u> answered is because we are *not* genuinely in His likeness nor in His character when we ask (even though we have attached the words "in His Name").

Also, could it be said that *carnal* Christians, like Pastor Bruce, would be "taking the Lord's Name in vain," which is the 3rd commandment in Exodus 20? Wow, that's a different way of looking at things. Isn't it? The concordance defines the word *vain* as falsehood or lying. In other words, when we do this we put up a false image of the One who created us. We give an erroneous, untrue, incorrect, wrong, misleading, false or phony impression. In the dictionary, it's actually called being *a traitor*!

***The bottom line is that just because we "possess" His Name does not mean we are "in" His Name.*** These two concepts are totally different. Just like "living in the Spirit" does not necessarily mean we are "walking by the Spirit."

The Lord wants His Name to be exalted not just with our words, but also with our lives.[50]   His Name is of the utmost importance to Him. And thus, we must strive to make it be remembered in all generations. (Psalm 45: 17) We do this simply by glorifying Him in all we think, say and do.

Salvation, then, is then summed up in Jesus Name. (Acts 8:12) "Believe in His Name" from John 3:18 simply means *reveal the essence of Christ's person.* Psalm 96:2-3 and verse 8 explain it well: "Sing unto the Lord, bless His Name; shew forth His salvation from day to day. Declare His glory among the heathen, His wonders among all people...*Give unto the Lord the glory due unto His Name.*"[51]

Do you personally do this?

*Suffering for His Name* simply means holding fast to His character, His essence and His image even in the most difficult of circumstances and barring ourselves from following anything or anyone that would deter us from that.[52]   God's glory is verbalized by means of His Name. (Exodus 33:18-34) ***His "Name," therefore, is the***

---

50      Isaiah 12:4; Psalm 91
51      1 John 3:23; Deuteronomy 12:5,11,21; 14:23; 16:2,6; 2 Samuel 7:13
52      Isaiah 24:15; 1 Peter 4:14-16; Revelation 2:3

***motive for our service, but His "glory" is the message.***[53] His essence is only shown forth only when we are "in His Name." (Acts 3:16; 4:12)

"I will praise Thee, O Lord my God, with all my heart: and I will glorify Thy Name for evermore. (Psalm 86:12) "You are the health of my countenance." (Psalm 43:5; 89:17)

Only as we choose to *follow the leading of the Spirit, be cleansed by the Spirit, worship in the Spirit, abide in the Spirit and, then, walk by the Spirit,* will we ever be able, like that one leper in Luke 17, to turn back and glorify the Lord in all that we do. (Verses 12-18)

Being **reflections of His image**, therefore, is the purpose of our lives!

---

**"To the end that my glory may sing praise to You and not be silent."** (Psalm 30:12)

---

[53]     From *Dictionary of the Later New Testament* by Ralph Martin.

# Chapter Eight Questions

1) Scripture seems to suggest that the greater the suffering, the greater the glory. And, it gives Jesus as our example. Can you explain. (Acts 14:22; John 12:24-25; Isaiah 53:5, 7, 10)

2) We are to be "mirror images" of Christ. What exactly does this mean? (Matthew 5:44; Isaiah 42:12; Psalm 45:17)

3) The chief objective of man, then, is to do what? Why? (2 Corinthians 3:18; Psalm 29:2; 96:7-8)

4) Seeing the glory of God in believers is the key to revival. Why?

5) Jesus lived a life of serving. If we truly want to glorify God, what must we do? (Matthew 20:26-27)

6) Much of the Christian body today are like "candles hidden under bushels." Why? (Luke 11:33-34)

7) What are some of the blessings that will occur when we learn to "walk after the Spirit" and glorify God?

8) Why must Christ's Name always precede any blessings? What does His Name really mean? (2 Corinthians 3:17)

9) Why aren't our prayers not answered when we've said the words "in Jesus' Name"?

10) His Name is the *motive* for our service, but His glory is the _____?

# Bibliography

**Bibles:**

Scofield, C.I., *The Holy Bible*, King James
   Version, Oxford University Press, N.Y. 1969.
*The Companion Bible*, King James Version,
   Zondervan, Grand Rapids, Mi., 1974.
*The Interlinear Bible*, Hebrew, Greek, English,
   Associated Publishers, Wilmington, Delaware,
   1976.
*The Septuagint Version*, Greek and English, Sir
   Lancelot C.L. Brenton, Zondervan, Grand
   Rapids, Mi. 1970.

**Technical Helps:**

Bahat, Dan, *Touching the Stones of Our Heritage*,
   The Western Wall Heritage Foundation,
   Jerusalem, 2002.
Bagster, Samuel, *The Holy Vessels and Furniture of
   the Tabernacle of Israel,* London, England (late
   1800's).
Blackhouse, Robert, *The Jerusalem Temple*,
   Candle Books, Carlisle, Cambria.
Botterweck, G. Johannes & Helmer Ringgren,
   *Theological Dictionary of the Old Testament,*
   Eerdmans, Grand Rapids, 1974.

Cutman, J., *The Temple of Solomon*, Scholars Press, Missoula, Montana, 1976.

*Encyclopedia Judaica* (16 Vol), Keter Publishing House, Jerusalem, Israel.

Edershem, Alfred, *The Temple: It's Ministry and Services,* Hendrickson Publishers, Peabody, Massachusetts, 1994.

Garrard, A.W., *The Splendor of the Temple*, Suffolk, England, 1997.

*International Standard Bible Encyclopedia,* Eerdmans, Grand Rapids, Mich. 1976.

Luzzatto, Rabbi Moshe Chaim, *Secrets of the Future Temple*, The Temple Institute, Jerusalem, 1999.

Martin, Ralph, *Dictionary of Later New Testament*, InterVarsity Press, Illinois, 1997.

*The Pulpit Commentary,* Eerdmans, Grand Rapids, 1963.

Richman, Chaim, *The Holy Temple of Jerusalem*, The Temple Institute, Jerusalem, 1997.

Richman, Chaim, *The Light of the Temple*, The Temple Institute, Jerusalem.

Soltau, Henry W., *The Holy Vessels and Furniture of the Tabernacle,* Kregel Publications, Grand Rapids, Mich.

Starrett, Yehoshua, *The Inner Temple*, Breslov Research Institute, Jerusalem/N.Y., 2000.

Strong, James, *Strong's Expanded*, Thomas Nelson, Nashville, Tenn., 2001.

*The Pulpit Commentary*, Eerdmans, Volume 17,
Grand Rapids, 1963.

*Theological Dictionary of the New Testament,*
Eerdmans, Grand Rapids, Mi. 1976.

Unger, Merrill, *Unger's New Bible Dictionary,*
R.K. Harrison Edition, Moody Press,
Chicago, Illinois.

Vine, W.E., *The Expanded Vines*, Bethany House,
Minneapolis, Minn.,1984.

**All other references from:**

Allen, Ronald B., *The Wonder of Worship*,
Word Publishing, Nashville, Tenn., 2001.

Barna, George, *Experience God in Worship*,
Group Publishing, Loveland, Co., 2000.

Cornwell, Judson, *Forbidden Glory*, McDougal
Publishing, Hagerstoon, N.D., 2001.

Cornwell, Judson, *Let Us Abide*, Bridge
Publishing, So. Planfield, N.J., 1977.

Cornwell, Judson, *Things We Adore*, Destiny
Image Publishers, Shippensbury, Pa. 1991.

Cornwell, Judson, *David Worship a Living God*,
Destiny Image Publishers, Shippensbury,
Pa., 1998.

Crabb, Larry, *Inside Out.*

Edwards, Gene, *The Highest Life*,
Tyndale House, Wheaton, Illinois, 1991.

Govett, Robert, *Is Sanctification Perfect Here Below?,* Conley and Schoettle Publishing Co., Miami Springs, Fla., 1985.

Hayford, Jack, *Worship His Majesty*, Regal Books, Ventura, California, 2000.

Hayford, Jack, *Pursuing the Will of God*, Multnomah Books, Sisters, Or., 1997.

Kraeuter, Tom, *Worship is What?*, Emerald Books, Lynwood, Washington 1996.

Martin, Ralph, *The Worship of God*, Eerdmans Publishers, Grand Rapids, Mi. 1982.

Mathias, Art, *In His Image*, Wellspring Publishing, Anchorage, Alaska.

Mathias, Art, *Biblical Foundations of Freedom,* Wellspring Publishing, Anchorage, Alaska.

Missler, Nancy, *Private Worship: The Key to Joy*, The King's High Way Ministries, CdA, Idaho, 2002.

Missler, Nancy *The Way of Agape*, The King's High Way Ministries, CdA, Idaho, 1995.

Missler, Nancy, *Be Ye Transformed*, The King's High Way Ministries, CdA, Idaho, 1996.

Morey, Robert, *Worship, Not Just Sunday Morning*, World Bible Publishing, Iowa Falls, Iowa, 2001.

Mueller, George, *Autobiography of George Mueller*, Whitaker House, New Kensington, Pennsylvania.

Murray, Andrew, *Full Life in Christ*, Whitaker House, New Kensington, Pa. 2000.

Needham, David, *Birthright*, Multnomah Press, Portland, Or. 1985.

Nee, Watchman, *The Spiritual Man*, Christian Fellowship Publishers, N.V., 1968.

Packer, J.I., *Keep in Step with the Spirit*, Baker Books, Grand Rapids, Michigan, 2005.

Peterson, David, *Engaging with God*, InterVarsity Press, Downers Grove, Ill., 1992.

Price, Randall, *The Temple and Bible Prophesy,* Harvest House Publishers, Eugene, Oregon, 2005.

Powell, Graham, *Christian, Set yourself Free*

Sanders, J. Oswald, *Enjoying Intimacy with God,* Moody Press, Chicago, Ill., 1980.

Shankle, Randy, *Merismos*, Whitaker House, Springdale, PA., 1987.

Shankle, Randy, *Releasing the Spirit,* Whitaker House, Springdale, PA., 1987.

Spurgeon, Charles, *Spiritual Warfare in a Believer's Life*, Emerald Books, Lynwood, Washington, 1993.

Wilkins, Michael J., *In His Image*, Nav Press, Colorado Springs, Colorado, 1997.

**All other sources:**

Internet: Solomon's Temple, *International Bible Standard Encyclopedia,*
Internet: Solomon's Temple, *New Bible Dictionary*
Internet: Temple, *Fausset's Bible Dictionary*

Internet: Temple, *Easton's Bible Dictionary*

Internet: www.firestone.org., "Crisis in Leadership"
Internet: www.maranthalife.com,. "Life Line
    for Pastors"
Internet: www.bibleteacher.org., "The Key
    to Glorifying God"
Internet: www.discoverthebook.org., "Jesus - I am
    the Vine"
Internet: www.faithbibleohio.com., "Glorifying
    God," by Chuck Long
Internet: www.gospelmessage.net., "Glorifying
    God"
Internet: www.bibletopics.com., "Glorifying God"
Internet: www.christmylife.org., "Glorifying God"
Internet: www.reformed.org., Westminister Larger
    Catechism
Internet: www.revivaltheology.com., "Glorifying
    God," Lecture by Rev. Charles G. Finney, 1839
Internet: www.religioustolerance.org., "U.S.
    divorce Rates for Faith Groups"

**Article:** Ron Sider, "*The Scandal of Evangelical
Conscious*," Christianity Today, April 2005.

**Video Series:** Dr. Bruce Thompson,
    *God's Divine Plumbline*, 1985.

**Newsletters:** David Wilkerson, *"The Effects of Seeing the Glory of God,"* World Challenge, Inc., Lindale, Texas.

David Wilkerson, *"Called to be Christ-like,"* ibid, April, 2005.

David Wilkerson, *"Seeking the Face of God,"* ibid, November 2005.

KHW

# What is The King's High Way?

The King's *High* Way is a ministry dedicated to encouraging and teaching Christians how to walk out their faith, i.e., focusing on the practical application of Biblical principles. Our passion is to help believers learn how to love as Jesus loved; how to renew their minds so their lives can be transformed; and, how to have unshakeable faith in their night seasons. Isaiah 62:10 is our commission: helping believers walk on the King's High Way by gathering out the stumbling blocks and lifting up the banner of Jesus.

For more information, please write to:

The King's *High* Way
P.O. Box 3111
Coeur d' Alene, Idaho 83816

or call:
# 1-866-775-KING

On the Internet:
http://www.kingshighway.org

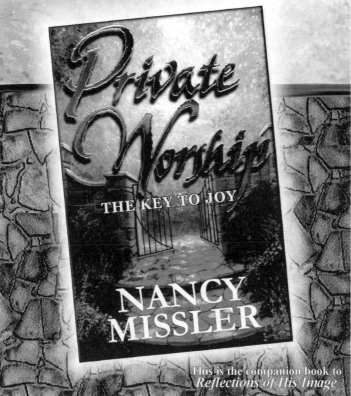

KHW

FAITH In The Night Seasons
UNDERSTANDING GOD'S WILL

CHUCK & NANCY MISSLER

Faith in the Night Seasons

# UNDERSTANDING GOD"S WILL

Speaking from personal experience, Chuck and Nancy share the details of their own devastating "night season"--bankruptcy, the loss of their home and friends, a 6.8 earthquake under their rented home, and finally, the unexpected death of their son. They not only tell their own story, but go on to explain why God allows times like these and what we are to do in them.

**Additional Resources:**
Textbook
Personal Application Workbook
Audiotape Series (8 hours)
Videotape Series (7 sessions)
DVD Series (7 sessions)
DVD Bible Study Package
Leader's Guide

# 1-866-775-KING

On the Internet:
http://www.kingshighway.org

KHW

# Plain & Simple Series

### The Key - HOW TO LET GO AND LET GOD

This book teaches us the moment-by-moment steps to letting go of ourselves, our circumstances and others and putting on Christ. It gives us a practical guide to giving our problems to God and leaving them there. This is one of our most popular books.

## Why Should I be the Frist to Change?
### THE KEY TO A LOVING MARRIAGE

This is the story of the amazing "turnaround" of Chuck and Nancy's 20-year Christian marriage which reveals the dynamic secret that releases the power of God's Love already resident in every believer. Riveting, yet easy reading.

### Tomorrow May Be Too Late
#### DISCOVERING OUR DESTINY

A simple, non-threatening and easy to read book that chronicles God's whole plan for mankind. In just a little over a hundred pages, it relates man's spiritual journey from the beginning of time to the very end, showing how God has been personally and intimately involved all along. Perfect for non-believers.

### The Choice - HYPOCRISY OR REAL CHRISTIANITY

As Christians, we are faced with a constant choice: either to live our Christian life in our own power and ability, or to set ourselves aside and let Christ live His Life out through us. Written especially for youth.

### Against the Tide
#### GETTING BEYOND OURSELVES

This little book gives the practical tools we need to implement "faith choices" in our lives. These are choices that set aside our natural thoughts and emotions, and allow us to love and be loved as God desires. Great for understanding our emotions.

### Never Give Up! - THE FRUIT OF LONGSUFFERING

Most of us talk very openly about the need to "be like Christ" and to have His characteristics of Love, joy, peace, but what about the fruit of longsuffering—the determination never to give up? God promises us that He will strengthen us; help us and uphold us. (Isaiah 41:10) The question is: How do we, like Paul, patiently endure our trials? This little book gives us the answers!